DAILY DEVOTIONS

DAILY DEVOTIONS

S. Rickly Christian

ZondervanPublishingHouse
Grand Rapids, Michigan

A Division of HarperCollins*Publishers*

Alive 1
Copyright © 1983, 1995 by S. Rickly Christian

Requests for information should be addressed to:

ZondervanPublishingHouse
Grand Rapids, Michigan 49530

Library of Congress Cataloging-in-Publication Data
Christian, S. Rickly (Scott Rickly)
    Alive 1 : daily devotions / S. Rickly Christian.—Rev. ed.
      p.   cm.
    Rev. ed. of: Alive!, ©1983.
    Summary: Daily readings for high school students, using Scripture as a
springboard to reflect on God and Christianity in school life, dating, sex, parental
relations, fears, peer pressure, and more.
    ISBN: 0-310-49901-1 (softcover)
    1. Teenagers—Prayer-books and devotions—English.   2. Devotional calendars.
[1. Prayer books and devotions. 2. Christian life.]   I. Christian, S. Rickly (Scott
Rickly) Alive! II. Title.
BV4850.C53   1995
242'.6—dc 20   95-16463
                                                       CIP
                                                       AC

Cover design by Paula Gibson
Interior design by Sue Koppenol

*Interior photos on pages 29, 63, 151, 173, 197, 209, 219, and 267 by H. Armstrong
Roberts, Inc. All other interior photos by Cleo Freelance Photography.*

Printed in the United States of America

99 00 01 02 /❖ DC/ 15 14 13

For Julie
Don't let anyone look down on you
because you are young,
but set an example . . . in speech,
in life, in love, in faith, and in purity.

CONTENTS

INTRODUCTION

The teen years consist of acne, smelly gym clothes, Friday-night football games, first loves, broken romances, cruddy jobs, and stab-in-the-back gossip. Youth is a period—through which everyone passes—marked by a unique blend of hilarity and agony, accomplishment and embarrassment, bravado and desperation. But perhaps more than anything else, the teen years are a time of facing the challenge of life's first tough decisions.

After graduation, most people ruefully admit they'd give anything for the chance to go back and relive those years . . . but with the advantage of hindsight. However, you can't go back. To paraphrase Longfellow, the teen years come but once in a lifetime.

As a young Christian, I wanted God to be part of those "once-in-a-lifetime" years. Not just any part. The biggest part. Trouble is, I fell asleep a lot while reading my Bible. Christians whom I respected used daily devotionals to help spark their quiet time alone with the Lord. So I followed their example and raided the nearby Christian bookstore.

However, the devotionals I bought were far removed from the unique pressures I faced at that age. The classics, such as Oswald Chambers' *My Utmost for His Highest*, were too heady and verbose. Others were jammed with illustrations that older adults might appreciate—stories about the world wars, depression years, Napoleon, etc.—but which sounded to me like boring history lectures. I found devotionals for expectant mothers, young fathers, housewives, families, pastors, and children. But I could find nothing practical that *I* could readily relate to.

It was with that need in mind that I wrote *Alive 1* and its sequel, *Alive 2*. Each book contains daily readings for about half a year. The readings begin with a passage from Scripture as a springboard to reflect on God and Christianity in the context of such things as campus life, peer pressure, dating and sex, demanding parents,

15

minimum-wage budgets, and fears about life after graduation. Several Bible passages are then suggested for further reading and study.

Alive and *Alive 2* are neither "preachy" nor condescending. Their tone is relevant, their language to the point. They discuss real life without cover-up or pretense.

As we all know, real life is often filled with discouragement and despair. We've fallen for the hype; what we need is hope. This book is full of encouragement for people like us. On the following pages, you'll find help for everyday realities. And you'll hear about the person whose life communicated the ultimate message of hope: that God cares about your own "once-in-a-lifetime" years.

One final word. Everyone wonders about my name. It's real. My only excuse for it is that my mother named me funny. The "S" stands for Scott, but I never used it because my father had prior claim to that name and we figured things would get confusing around the house. "Rickly" is my mother's maiden name. My friends all call me Rick. And it's fine with me if you do, too.

S. Rickly Christian
Colorado Springs, Colorado

THE PERSONAL TAG

Rejoice that your names are written in heaven.

LUKE 10:20

I have a strange habit. Whenever I travel, the first thing I do upon checking into a hotel or stopping for gas is to open the local phone book. I want to know whether anyone else has my name. So far, no one has. But then, I have an unusual name: S. Rickly Christian.

That name, assigned by my parents, was written on a blue plastic bracelet and attached to my arm shortly after birth. These bracelets, given to all babies, were the hospital's way of ensuring that newborns wouldn't accidentally get switched.

Later, that name was the first word I learned to scribble with crayons. It became the name my friends used when they shouted for me down a crowded locker hall; the name my coach bellowed when I didn't swim fast enough; the name my girlfriend whispered in my ear, causing goose bumps on my neck.

More than any other label, my name symbolizes who I am: my personality, my dreams, my failures, my successes. And it's such a personal tag that my ears pop when I hear my name mentioned in conversation.

To know that my name, according to Luke, is a matter of celestial chitchat causes my *mind* to pop! Are you sure, Luke? My *name* recorded in God's Book of Life? I suppose God could keep roll more efficiently by using my social security number or bank access code. Numbers are easier to program, but God evidently prefers to use names.

That preference, I think, reflects the kind of personal relationship he wants to build with me. It's his way of assuring me that I matter; I'm not just some insignificant blip or digit code in the far corner of the universe.

Perhaps that is why the Bible is so full of long genealogies—God didn't want to miss a single name!

God's use of my name also signals his concern for the things my name represents: everything from my biggest hurts to my highest hopes. My name in my yearbook reminds my friends of such things as the day we shared together at the beach, the time we cried when we learned of another friend's cancer, the times we belly-laughed at a good joke.

My name, I believe, triggers the same kinds of memories in God's mind: the times we talked together in prayer, the time he comforted me during my mom's illness, the time I was dazzled by the splash of color he gave a peacock.

Looking back, those were special times, times of getting to know each other on a first-name basis.

See also: 1 Chronicles 1–9; Matthew 1:1–17

"THEY SAID ..."   7/31/00

Consider what a great forest is set on fire by a small spark. The tongue also is a fire, a world of evil among the parts of the body. It corrupts the whole person, sets the whole course of his life on fire, and is itself set on fire by hell.

JAMES 3:5–6

A few years ago, officials at McDonald's headquarters in Oak Brook, Illinois, became very sensitive about the topic of *earthworms.*

If you had mentioned the subject in the office, chances were good you'd have been tackled by a wart-faced fry cook and gagged with a half-dozen sesame seed buns. The reason: Ronald McDonald and his Golden Arch cohorts were fighting a rumor that they used the creepy crawlers as protein substitute in their burgers.

The rumor spread across America like ... well, like earth-worms after a spring rain. Sales slumped, and the king of the burger was forced to launch a lavish campaign to regain its reputation.

Rumors usually don't reach such proportions. Often they just circulate among a close circle of friends in places like school locker halls and cafeterias. And generally the rumors damage lives and individual reputations, not those of corporations.

Such was the case when the new girl moved to town from Florida. Other girls at school felt threatened. They didn't have her cover-girl looks or *Seventeen* wardrobe. So they protected them-selves by talking behind her back.

"You're kidding! I never knew *that*," said one girl. And before long tongues were wagging all over campus. To make the story *really* juicy, they'd pad the tale a little here, stretch a bit there. Soon, this poor girl's life was on the rocks—shipwrecked.

The anguish she must have felt and tears she must have cried are probably similar to a case I read about in which a woman's suicide note simply read, "They said ..."

She didn't complete the sentence. Something "They said" killed her.

See also: Psalm 140:1–3; Romans 1:29–32; 1 Peter 3:8–12

THE EXCHANGE   8/1/00

I pray that you, being rooted and established in love, may have power, together with all the saints, to grasp how wide and long and high and deep is the love of Christ.

EPHESIANS 3:17–18

Imagine this scene. You've just been born and are taking your first breaths outside your mother's womb. The obstetrician and nurse are smiling, but your parents are strangely smug. They confer quietly to themselves, ignoring your cries.

"Doctor," your father says, turning to the physician, "would you mind holding the baby up again so we can better decide?"

"Decide what?" the doctor asks, lifting you up into the light.

"We just want to be sure the child's *right* for us," your father says. "We saw another baby in the nursery that seemed to have, well, a little more promise. This one here is too ruddy, and the eyes are the wrong color. We wanted a child with blue eyes and, you know, a shorter nose."

He whispers something in your mother's ear, and then motions the obstetrician closer.

"Doctor, I'm sure we could eventually learn to love this little one, but we have our hearts set on that cute blond baby. My wife and I have discussed this, and we'd like to work out an exchange. The hospital said we could pay the transfer fee with our Visa card."

This scenario is understandably absurd. When you were born, your parents accepted you into their family without qualifications. Their love was not based on your looks or performance. Not even your drooling mattered. They loved you simply because you were their child. Granted, their love at times was not perfect. There were times they withheld their affection—like the time you wrecked the family car or the night you missed your curfew by three hours. So while a parent's love is great, it does have limits.

But God's love has no bounds. You're loved because you're his child, and nothing you ever do will make him love you any more or less. His love is unconditional. As the apostle Paul wrote, "Neither death nor life, neither angels nor demons, neither the present nor the future, nor any powers, neither height nor depth, nor anything else in all creation, will be able to separate us from the love of God that is in Christ Jesus our Lord" (Rom. 8:38–39).

When you realize you're loved that much, you begin to feel like you're worth loving ... and begin loving others in the same way, because God loves even the most unlovable as much as he loves you.

See also: Romans 8:31–39; 1 John 4:19–21

CARBON COPYING   8/2/00

> *If anyone is in Christ, he is a new creation; the old has gone, the new has come!*
>
> 2 CORINTHIANS 5:17

I always thought of myself as a lot like Frank. Or maybe I just tried to be like him. When he went out for the swim team, I went out for the swim team. When he dropped that for the tennis team, I was right behind him.

We were both journalism junkies and wrote for the school paper. We both got involved in student-body politics. We liked the same kind of music, disliked the same teachers for the same reasons, wore the same style of jeans, went to the same parties, body-surfed at the same beach, and even dated some of the same girls.

But things began to change when I became a Christian. I decided to let God take control of my life, and I thought Frank eventually would, too. But that never happened. The "big" questions about life that drew me closer to God—Why do I exist? What happens after death? Were Jesus' claims valid? What purpose is there in life?—didn't seem to phase Frank.

When I'd try to talk to him about these things, he'd brush me off. "You're getting all philosophical, and it's just not where I'm at," he'd say. End of conversation.

Slowly I began to notice we were going in different directions. Parties that once seemed fun began feeling like an empty waste of time. Getting drunk seemed pointless. Jokes I once thought were funny seemed crude and prejudiced—the laugh was always at someone else's expense.

God began to instill in me value for other people. They took on new importance because of *who* they were (unique creations of God) rather than for *what* they were (good-looking, smart, funny, etc.). Members of the opposite sex became more than just "bodies." My parents and teachers became more than just authorities. In them I discovered people with many of the same needs I had—but I'd never noticed before.

When I think of Frank, I feel how a pardoned criminal probably feels toward buddies left behind in prison. You'd love for them to join you on the outside, yet the bars are all they know. And they only laugh when you tell them that the warrant for release—the pardon—has already been signed.

Becoming a Christian is an acceptance of that fact. It's not an effort, a striving, a ceaseless seeking, as one writer said. It's a letting go. And slowly you begin to notice that Christ is working on you from the inside out to give you new purpose, new values ... and a new pattern for life.

See also: Ephesians 4:17–24; 6:10–18

THE VISIBILITY FACTOR

A city on a hill cannot be hidden. Neither do people light a lamp and put it under a bowl. Instead they put it on its stand, and it gives light to everyone in the house. In the same way, let your light shine before men, that they may see your good deeds and praise your Father in heaven.

MATTHEW 5:14–16

Melinda was a typical case of what John Stott calls a "rab-bit-hole Christian." She'd bounce out her front door in the morning after a mere grunt at her parents, scurry to school, and then race from the parking lot looking for her usual clique of Christian friends. Their favorite hangout before class: a bank of lockers, plastered with Christian stickers.

When the bell rang, she'd proceed with her holy huddle to journalism, where they'd sit together in the back corner by the window. Often they'd pass notes back and forth and giggle quietly about some hidden joke. When lunch arrived, Melinda would make a mad dash to the cafeteria and lay her books and sweater across a large table to reserve it for other Christians. They'd talk about God and how messed up their families were, and then retreat outside together for some informal Bible reading on the lawn.

After class, she'd buzz home, snort dinner, and then drive across town to pick up fellow Christians, sometimes for a Bible study at church, where they'd pray for God's help in witnessing to nonbelievers at school. After the final prayers, she'd scurry back home, wave to her parents in passing, and then disappear into her room where she'd mumble a few "bless 'ems" before falling asleep. And upon waking in the morning, she would begin her harried, holy pace all over again.

As Christians, we can't be lights of the world if our only contacts with unbelievers are those mad blitzes to and from Christian gatherings. We can't withdraw—we must penetrate darkness with the light of God's love. And it's hard to generate much brightness from rabbit holes.

See also: Matthew 28:18–20; Mark 1:17; John 8:12

HOLY HYPE 8/3

> *If anyone considers himself religious and yet does not keep a tight rein on his tongue, he deceives himself and his religion is worthless.*
>
> JAMES 1:26

I earned decent grades in most classes, but was less than a scholar with foreign languages. I took three years of Spanish in high school, yet scored 17 out of 150 points on a college proficiency test. And if I tried to converse with a native in Tijuana today, I probably couldn't get much further than ¿Como tu frijole? *How you bean?*

I switched to French in college. The result? I can count to ten, barely, and can pronounce "lingerie," "crepe," and "toilet" without looking in a dictionary. In other languages I can, let's see ... say "love you" in Tagalog and Japanese; I can remember a few words in Italian like "spaghetti," "ravioli," and "lasagna"; and I can hold my own in Australia, Ireland, and Kentucky, though the foreign accents trouble me.

With such a background, I sympathize with people who understandably scratch their heads when Christians convene their holy huddles and start rambling about things like redemption, agape love, trinity, rapture, and being saved by the blood.

One writer has said the world is bombarded with a mishmash of religious gobbledygook from people like "Theodore Theologian" with his pointy-headed talk about glorification, justification, and sanctification ... and his counterpart, "Rev. Pat Popcorn," with his holy hype about "Praise Gawd! Jump for joy! I see those hands! Pass the plate! Amen!"

Actions speak louder than words, it is said. Perhaps that is why the apostle Peter, in writing to Christian women married to unbelievers, urged the wives to let their godliness be demonstrated by their lives, not their words: "They [the husbands] may be won over *without words* by the behavior of their wives."

The apostle James was adamant that Christians "keep a tight rein on their tongues"—that they be "slow to speak" and instead show their faith by good life and deeds.

You see, it's much easier to *sound* spiritual and gush "Praise the Lord!" than it is to *be* spiritual. That's the problem Christ found with the Pharisees, religious leaders who talked godly but lived godlessly.

With that in mind, try an experiment: See what happens when you stop just *telling* people you're a Christian and start *showing* them. It can be a very radical way of living.

See also: 1 Peter 3:1; James 3:13; 1 John 3:18

▦

POINTS TO PONDER–CHRISTIANITY

You are the light of the world.

MATTHEW 5:14

If you were arrested for being a Christian, would there be enough evidence to convict you?

DAVID OTIS FULLER

A person may go to heaven without health, without riches, without honors, without learning, without friends; but he can never go there without Christ.

JOHN DYER

He is no fool who gives what he cannot keep to gain what he cannot lose.

JIM ELLIOT

There is one single fact which we may oppose to all the wit and argument of infidelity, namely, that no man ever repented of being a Christian on his death bed.

HANNAH MORE

The trouble with some of us is that we have been inoculated with small doses of Christianity which keep us from catching the real thing.

LESLIE DIXON WEATHERHEAD

It is so hard to believe because it is so hard to obey.

SÖREN KIERKEGAARD

If your father and mother, your sister and brother, if the very cat and dog in the house, are not happier for your being Christian, it is a question whether you really are.

HUDSON TAYLOR

Christian: one who believes that the New Testament is a divinely inspired book admirably suited to the spiritual needs of his neighbors.

AMBROSE BIERCE

Jesus Christ will never strong-arm his way into your life.

GRADY B. WILSON

Being a Christian is more than just an instantaneous conversion—it is a daily process whereby you grow to be more and more like Christ. Jesus Christ is the man God wants every man to be like.

BILLY GRAHAM

Christianity is the land of beginning again.

W. A. CRISWELL

Those who live in the Lord never see each other for the last time.

GERMAN MOTTO

A Christian is one who is on [Christ's] way, though not necessarily very far along it, and who has at least some dim and half-baked idea of whom to thank. A Christian isn't necessarily any nicer than anybody else. Just better informed.

FREDERICK BUECHNER

Take the case of a sour old maid, who is a Christian, but cantankerous. On the other hand, take some pleasant and popular fellow, but who has never been to Church. Who knows how much more cantankerous the old maid might be if she were *not* a Christian, and how much more likable the nice fellow might be if he *were* a Christian? You can't judge Christianity simply by comparing the *product* in these two people; you would need to know what kind of raw material Christ was working on in both cases.

C. S. LEWIS

When a Christian is in the wrong place, his right place is empty.

T. J. BACH

See also: Matthew 5:13; Colossians 3:1–17

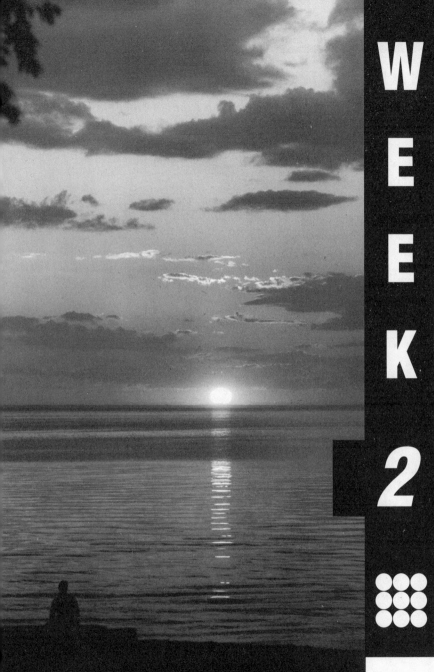

WEEK 2

SOUNDS OF SILENCE

Be still before the Lord and wait patiently for him.

PSALM 37:7

Yesterday, O Lord, was a frantic day—
  of running and driving and chasing;
    A 24-hour blur of sights and sounds.
Your calm, Your still, small voice
Was drowned by the rumble of traffic,
  The boom of stereo loudspeakers,
    The drone of gossip,
      The blast of coaches' whistles,
        The scream of family arguments,
  The blare of prime-time television,
    The ring of telephones,
      The crash of locker doors,
        The pound of headaches that beat like bass drums.
Lost in the circus of sounds, O Lord,
Was Your golden voice that was meant to whisper
  Your comfort as softly as a forest breeze,
    As softly as a kitten's purr, a lover's kiss, a child's embrace.
Buried amidst the cacophony of noise, O Lord,
Was Your calm assurance that was intended to come
  As silently as a cloud sailing the sky,
    As silently as a smile, a ray of light, a bird in flight.
Help me today to rediscover Your nearness—
  To quiet my soul and hear You speak,
    To shut out the high-decibel sounds of people, and traffic,
and music;

That I may again hear the sounds of Your silence
So deep, deep within my heart.

See also: Psalm 46:10; 131:2; Isaiah 32:17; Zephaniah 3:17

PEER PRESSURE 8/6

> *Do not conform any longer to the pattern of this*
> *world, but be transformed by the renewing of your mind.*
>
> ROMANS 12:2

Mark was the kind of guy you loved to hate. He wore wingtip shoes and sport coats to class, played electronic chess during lunch, published research papers on sixteenth-century Huguenots in history journals, and debated the science teacher about obscure textbook facts.

Everyone figured he'd be the school valedictorian, attend an Ivy League university, and win the Nobel Prize or something similar down the road.

But that never happened. In his junior year, Mark got tired of everyone thinking he was different from them. He wanted friends to hang around with, friends to joke with, friends to go to parties with. He wanted to be just a regular guy. And in his mind, regular meant drinking, smoking, fast cars, and fast girls.

It was really a surprise when Mark showed up at a basketball game drunk. And he created shock waves among faculty members when he was suspended for smoking pot in the bathroom. He started playing dumb in class, exchanged his calculator for a pack of Marlboros, and studied Zen instead of Huguenots and inert gases.

Even though I'd resented Mark for distorting the class grading curves, I felt sad watching him succumb to peer pressure. He quickly became just another face in the crowd. I kept hoping he'd come around and regain his sense of individuality, but that never

31

happened. He never took the SAT college entrance exam, and Arlene Schneider beat him out as valedictorian. (Actually it wasn't even close. He dropped to the 38th position in our graduating class.)

Instead of pursuing a brilliant career, he took a job at a beach snack shop. And whenever I think of peer pressure and its effects, I think of Mark sitting in his stand, selling rainbow-colored snow cones for a buck twenty-five.

See also: Galatians 5:16–26; 6:7–10; 1 Peter 1:13–16

5:22 Fruits of the Spirit – love, joy, peace, patience, kindness, goodness, faithfulness, gentleness, self-control

THE LONELINESS DISEASE *8/7*

Be devoted to one another in brotherly love.

ROMANS 12:10

Anne thought there was something wrong with her. There was. She had the loneliness disease.

She probably had dozens of friends, but often moped about how she never dated and led a genuinely boring life compared with _____. She filled in the blank with any number of people.

Everyone knew why Anne didn't have close friends. It was because she constantly jabbered about her loneliness. The result: She was as depressing to be around as late-night talk radio.

Loneliness, I suppose, is one of the inevitable facts of being human. We all feel it: standing in line surrounded by unfamiliar faces; waiting for the phone to ring; leaving home. Even in a crowd of friends we can feel lonely. It's a universal feeling. But Anne thought it was some rare phenomenon that affected only her.

"The only way to have a friend," wrote Ralph Waldo Emerson, "is to be one." Somewhere along the line, Anne realized that principle. Over a period of months I noticed a change had come over her. She often ran errands for people, picked them up when their car was stranded, helped with their homework. She genuinely and lovingly *devoted* herself to others.

Later that year Anne started coming to workdays sponsored by our youth group. One such Saturday I spotted her atop a ladder with a bucket of paint. Her face was sunburned, and her hair was covered with blue Ultra Hide flat latex. But the most noticeable thing was her huge, bright smile. She had learned to reach out to others, thereby discovering the cure to her loneliness disease.

God reached out to us. Nowhere does the Bible say anyone beat a path to heaven to seek his friendship. Adam and Eve even hid from him. So Jesus took the first step toward us. He built a bridge where we had constructed walls. And his example, I believe, provides the guideline for us: "The only way to have a friend is to be one."

See also: Luke 6:38; Philippians 2:4

FUTURE FRENZY   8/8

> *"I know the plans I have for you,"* declares the Lord, *"plans to prosper you and not to harm you, plans to give you hope and a future."*
>
> JEREMIAH 29:11

Your best friend was accepted for the biochemistry program at Stanford University. Your brother was hired as special features writer for the local newspaper. Your girlfriend has an internship with the hospital.

Everyone you know is either going to college, working a good job, or getting married. It feels like you're the only person on Planet Earth who is honestly, desperately mixed up about the future.

Whenever your parents' friends come over, they always ask you the same question: "By the way, have you decided what you're going to *do?*"

You feel that same familiar pressure creeping over you, that knot of tension in your gut. Everyone expects you to know what you'll be doing for the rest of your life. But you don't even know what you'll be doing next year.

Thinking of the future can be scary. But the fear is not necessary. "When you worry, you pay interest on debts you don't owe," someone once said. That's especially true for Christians. God knows the desires of your heart and your uncertainties. And he promises not to leave you stranded without hope. You can relax in the knowledge that God has a unique plan for your life—a plan more fulfilling and a life more abundant than anything you could dream for yourself.

But his plan doesn't just happen by magic. You discover it as you draw closer to God each day. As you get to know him better and start making decisions affecting your future, his plans for your life will be made clear. He guarantees it.

See also: Psalm 37:4; 139:1–16

THE GREAT OBSCENITY 8|9

Watch out! Be on your guard against all kinds of greed; a man's life does not consist in the abundance of his possessions.

LUKE 12:15

The media bombardment began when you were barely beyond the goo-goo stage and still in diapers. If you were like most infants, one day you blurted out something profoundly silly, such as "Cocoa Puffs!"

It meant nothing to you—you were merely repeating something you'd heard during Saturday-morning cartoons. But your parents were so amused they bought you a box. And soon you were blurting other things, such as "Honey Comb!" and "Lucky Charms!"

Your desires have been greatly inflamed since then, thanks to media hucksters who create "need" for their products. To illustrate, when I recently heard a commercial for a new bubble gum, I thought, "Kid stuff!" Besides, chewing bubble gum makes my jaw ache. But the new product stuck in my mind, and I even caught myself singing the company's commercial jingle in the shower. Before long, my response changed from "How dumb!" into "Maybe it's not so dumb!" and then into "It's probably worth the money!" and finally into "I need some now!"

The problem is, the world teaches just the opposite of what Luke says in the verse above: your life *does* consist of your possessions. You see this when people try to define your life by the price of your clothes, the brand of your stereo, the age of your car, etc. Along the way, we're led to believe we need what we don't need at all. The result: Not only do we have many needless possessions, but our possessions have us.

When Jesus told us to store treasures in heaven rather than on earth, he added: "For where your treasure is, there your heart will be also" (Luke 12:34). As Richard Foster points out in *Freedom of Simplicity*, Christ wasn't saying your heart should or should not be where your treasure is; he was saying it *will* be.

At some point, we need to unplug today's propaganda machine that bombards us with the four-letter obscenity, "More!" And we need to discard the "shopping-cart attitude" toward life.

You might start by playing devil's advocate with today's commercials and advertisements. Will having that new pair of $95 shoes, the latest CD, or the "Super! New! Improved!" product really make you more popular, happy, and whole? Of course not. *Having* doesn't bring happiness—it just brings a desire to have more.

See also: Matthew 6:19–34

FRIENDS WHO GO BUMP

Let us not love with words or tongue but with actions and in truth.

1 JOHN 3:18

I was walking through the crowded locker hall when I felt a hand on my shoulder. Whipping around, I saw that it was Donna.

"Hey, did you hear about Jim?" she asked.

"What about him?" I'd just spent time with him the day before and things seemed okay. But as the news of his bust cascaded from her mouth, I shook my head. "No kidding! That doesn't even sound like Jim."

Jim was a close friend, at least as I measured closeness. We jogged together twice weekly, and had gone to school together since junior high. What was this talk now of drugs? The thought seemed insane. Maybe that's because I only knew the shell—the smiling, good-looking, always-joking Jim—but was oblivious to the subsurface erosion in his life. We'd never discussed our inner needs, doubts, or failings. So I naively assumed he didn't have any. Meanwhile, he was crumbling before my eyes.

Now that I think about it, that's pretty much how most of my friendships have been—nothing more than billiard-ball relationships. We would ricochet back and forth, but never connect in any meaningful way:

"How's it going?" *Bump.*

"Fine." *Bump.*

"Catch you later." *Bump.*

Somewhere along the line, friends become acquaintances—people to wave at, but not to get intimately involved with. We want to know what they're doing this weekend, but not about their needs and problems. When we ask how someone is doing, we *expect* a cursory "Fine!" or "Great!" or "Not bad, how about you?"

It's hard to imagine our reaction if someone instead responded, "Oh, pretty lousy actually. I woke up this morning not feeling much like a Christian. My parents were all over my back, and with the pressures I'm facing at school and work, I feel tempted to smoke some dope."

But that will never happen, because no one gets close enough to risk breaking through the high-gloss facades, to dare shattering the ceramic smiles. Nobody will burst into that inner shadow chamber where we sometimes think, feel, and act awfully desperate and very lonely. It's easier to wave and bump than to sit down and listen or confront.

The end result of all of this bumping is that we're appalled when someone stumbles and behaves like a real-life, imperfect human being. We act very surprised by their fall, and think it all happened overnight. But erosion of the heart is a slow process; we just never take time to notice.

See also: Hebrews 3:12–13; 10:24–25

THOSE "IMPOSSIBLE" POSSIBILITIES

> *I am the Lord, the God of all mankind. Is anything too hard for me?*
>
> JEREMIAH 32:27

For high school graduation, I was given an "indestructible" scuba-diving watch. It worked fine—until I accidentally smashed it.

Bits of the fluorescent hour and minute hands were jarred loose and jammed the inner workings. After that the watch never kept proper time. So I got a small screwdriver, pried the timepiece open, and began tinkering. That's when my *real* trouble began. Tiny gears soon littered the table—gears that are infinitely easier to take apart than put back together.

When I finally took the impossible mess to a specialist, his eyes popped. "What on earth have you *done?*" he asked, clucking his tongue. I just shrugged my shoulders and grinned sheepishly.

Our problem as Christians is that we hang onto our problems. This quirk isn't related only to mechanical things such as watches and cars—it's carried over into our everyday spiritual life as well. When problems hit, we probe and ponder, seeking our own solution. We worry and calculate. We simply don't go to the Specialist soon enough. When we finally turn the matter over to God, he gets the leftovers—the mishmash *left over* after our tinkering is done.

Yet the problems we fret most about are the very things we ought to trust God with. Nothing is too difficult for him.

"Yeah, but you don't know my situation," you think.

Reread the end of Jeremiah 32:27: "Is *anything* too hard for me?" Where you see the word "anything," substitute the concern you are carrying now. Fill in the blank: Is _____ too hard for me?

Your impossibility may be about finances or parents or feelings of inferiority or an old habit or your school plans next year or your job. A friendship healed, a bad memory erased, a sin forgiven, a family reconciled—*nothing* is too hard for the Lord.

Release your grip on your worries now. For as Christ said, "What is impossible with men is possible with God."

See also: Jeremiah 32:17; Luke 18:27

BETHLEHEM, USA

Your attitude should be the same as that of Christ Jesus: Who, being in very nature God, did not consider equality with God something to be grasped, but made himself nothing.

PHILIPPIANS 2:5–7

If Christ were reborn in the United States this month, I wonder how things would be different?

Would his birth warrant a blurb in *The New York Times*? Would CNN crews poke cameras in his face? Would an agent get him a Pampers commercial? Would he watch "Sesame Street" and "Mr. Rogers"?

Where would he grow up? In Malibu? In Boulder? In Boston? Or would he hang out in a Watts ghetto, just to be different? Would he attend a public school? A private academy? Or would he be home schooled by his parents? Would he go out for football or play in the band? Would he own the latest computer gizmo? Would he work after school and get yelled at by his boss?

Later on, where would he go to recruit his apostles? From corporate management programs? From Stanford Law School? From the wharf in San Francisco? Would he want you if you were black? Or gay? Or crippled?

Would he hold summer revival meetings and stay in Hiltons? Would he pass out tracts at beaches and airports? How would he respond to Hare Krishnas? To Southern Baptists? I wonder if he'd play pool in a bar? Would he come home at night and watch himself on the "CBS Evening News"?

Would he join a church? Become a pastor? How would he treat people with AIDS? And what would he wear: Levis with Nikes or an Armani suit with Italian loafers? Would he drive a truck or something red and fast? Would he fly first-class or coach?

I wonder if we'd recognize him? And if so, would we shout him down with racial slurs? Would we crucify him on an aluminum cross? Or would he get a life sentence and be paroled after seven years?

See also: Mark 10:35–45; John 13:1–17

FACE TO FACE

> *Jesus entered Jericho and was passing through. A man was there by the name of Zacchaeus; he was a chief tax collector and was wealthy. He wanted to see who Jesus was, but being a short man he could not, because of the crowd. So he ran ahead and climbed a sycamore-fig tree to see him, since Jesus was coming that way. When Jesus reached the spot, he looked up and said to him, "Zacchaeus, come down immediately. I must stay at your house today."*
>
> LUKE 19:1–5

The crowd was lined up three and four deep along the curb fronting Jericho's main drag, abuzz with anticipation as Jesus neared. On the edge of the parade throng, perched on tiptoes, stood Zacchaeus, a pint-sized swindler who was the district's IRS honcho. He was the kind of guy who, if he came through your front door, you'd run out the back—a man who, following the custom of his day, inflated people's tax bills and pocketed the difference.

From where he stood, craning his neck, Zacchaeus couldn't see a thing. So he shinnied up a tree for a better look, just as a wild roar rose from the streets. Suddenly Christ rounded the corner and stopped.

Distracted by a flash of bright clothing in the curbside tree, Jesus forgot about those on street level and turned his attention to Zacchaeus. You could have heard a pin drop. And when Jesus called for the crook to hop down, people could hardly wait for what would happen next. Jesus would probably make an example of Zacchaeus, as he did with the Pharisees: *You snake! You brood of vipers! You'll rot in hell!*

Zacchaeus knew better than anyone that that's what he deserved, and Jesus did, too. But that's not what happened. Jesus simply invited himself to be Zacchaeus's houseguest. Jumping from the tree, Zacchaeus pumped Christ's hand and blabbed excitedly about how he'd give half his belongings to Goodwill and pay people quadruple what he had cheated in tax surcharges. And that made Christ smile. But everyone else grumbled about how Jesus was berserk to even think of associating with someone like Zacchaeus.

Of course, Christ didn't think it was so crazy. After all, that's what usually happens when he meets sinners face-to-face. They receive just the opposite of what they deserve. The same thing happened to you and me. And that's what grace is all about. The world hasn't gotten over it yet.

See also: Romans 5:20; Ephesians 2:8–10; Revelation 3:20

SIDE BY SIDE

I will never leave you nor forsake you.

JOSHUA 1:5

I once read a story about a young man whose life was marked by repeated heartaches and discouragements. Several of his closest friends and family members died; his life goals were never attained; and financial trouble plagued him. Each day brought nothing but hardship and lonely times of crisis.

And then one night he had a vivid dream in which he saw himself walking along a windswept beach with the Lord. As they strode together against the gale, scenes from the young man's life flashed like lightning across the sky. Each scene, he noticed, was also depicted behind them in the sand as footprints—one set belonging to him, the other to the Savior.

When the last scene from the young man's life had lit up the evening sky, he turned and looked back at the ribbons of footprints crossing the shore. Something seemed odd. He dropped to his knees to examine the tracks more closely. Then he traced them back, remembering the scenes they corresponded with in his life.

Usually there was a double set of footprints, but at other times—often when he faced his biggest hardships—the second pair of footprints mysteriously disappeared. Confused, he turned to the Lord.

"I'm sorry, but none of this makes sense," he stammered. "We've walked together for a long time now, but I notice that during some of the roughest, most grueling moments of my life there is only one set of footprints in the sand. Why, Lord . . . ," he fumbled for words, "how could you desert my side when I needed you the most?"

"My dear, precious child," the Lord said, drawing the young man close to his body, "I promised I would never leave your side no matter what. The double set of footprints assures you of that."

"But . . . ," the young man began, pointing his finger behind him.

"When you look back and see just one pair of footprints," the Lord said, "it was then that I carried you."

See also: Psalm 23; 46; Matthew 11:28; John 14:27

THREE LOVES

> *You have heard that it was said, "Love your neighbor and hate your enemy." But I tell you: Love your enemies and pray for those who persecute you.*
>
> MATTHEW 5:43–44

"If love" is conditional love. It says, I love you . . .

if you run with the right crowd.

if you let me borrow your car this weekend.

if you will go to bed with me.

if you wear the latest styles and like loud music.

if you let me see your answers when I'm stumped.

if you don't hassle me with your problems.

if you loan me money for a pizza.

"Because love" is easy love. It says, I love you . . .

because you were "most-valuable player" in last week's game.

because you voted for me as class president.

because you're crazy and make me laugh.

because you throw wild parties and like rock 'n' roll.

because your character-reference letter helped me get accepted to college.

because you have a great body and nice hair.

because you are basically a lot like me.

"Anyhow love" is hard, unconditional love. It says, I love you . . .

anyhow, even if you ignore me when I talk.

anyhow, even if you judge me unfairly and gossip behind my back.

anyhow, even if you like classical music.

anyhow, even if you don't have a car.

anyhow, even if you have a fresh outbreak of acne.

anyhow, even if you grew up on the wrong side of the tracks.

anyhow, even if you don't understand me and my lifestyle.

Yes, I love you anyhow . . . because that's how God loves me. And I'm trying to learn to love you the same way.

See also: Luke 6:27–36; John 21:15–17; Philippians 2:1–4

SHOUT OF LOVE

Love is patient, love is kind. It does not envy, it does not boast, it is not proud. It is not rude, it is not self-seeking, it is not easily angered, it keeps no record of wrongs. Love does not delight in evil but rejoices with the truth. It always protects, always trusts, always hopes, always perseveres.

1 Corinthians 13:4–7

If I speak with the ease of a radio DJ and sing like a superstar, but don't have love, my words are like the grating whine of a woodshop buzz saw.

If I know my way through cyberspace and can program better than my computer teacher, if I memorize Genesis and can read Leviticus without falling asleep, or if I can even see the future and know everything about everything like some latter-day Wizard of Oz ... but have not love, my value to others is as sawdust.

If I donate my designer jeans to the Salvation Army and let my brother use my car, if I serve as a missionary to cannibals in Borneo, or if I give my body to science ... but don't have love, my contribution is worthless.

Love is patient—even if it means going to the beach with my mom or waiting quietly until my sister is finished primping in the bathroom.

Love is kind—it shares a table with the lonely boy at lunch and consoles the new girl who just moved to town from Kansas.

Love does not envy the student-body president, the hockey captain, the cheerleader, or even the blonde who has the world's most even tan.

Love doesn't boast about admittance to Harvard University or a science fair blue ribbon. Love isn't snooty about a new dress or a custom-built house on the right side of town.

Love doesn't jeer at the girl who weighs two hundred and plenty pounds and doesn't vie to be first in line. Love is cool as ice—even when provoked by the rival gang.

Love doesn't cheat when the teacher isn't looking or stop by the racks for a quick peek at *Penthouse* magazine. Love roots for what's right and shouts "Whoopee!" when the good guy wins. Love never quits.

Love isn't like a cheap stereo from the discount store. It never fails. Its power source is God, so it will last forever.

See also: John 3:16; John 13:34–35; 1 John 3:11–18

LOVE IS ...

Do everything in love.

1 CORINTHIANS 16:14

Love is one of those words that is difficult to define. Maybe that's because its meaning has become twisted over time.

You can say that you *love* your girlfriend or boyfriend ... but you can also say you *love* going to basketball games. You can *love* pizza, you can *love* gymnastics, you can *love* rock 'n' roll or a good movie. And then, you can *love* God.

But what is love? The apostle Paul did his best to define it in the so-called "Love Chapter" of 1 Corinthians 13. We read about that yesterday.

Try writing a few practical definitions of your own. Relate these definitions to people and things around you, your friends, and family. For example, you might say, "Love is the patience my friend displayed when I was late getting ready last Friday night." Or, "Love is the kindness I showed when I gave up my seat on the bus yester-day." Be original:

Love is ＿＿＿＿＿

Love is ＿＿＿＿＿

Love is ＿＿＿＿＿

Love is ＿＿＿＿＿

Love is ＿＿＿＿＿

Love is ＿＿＿＿＿

Love is ＿＿＿＿＿

See also: Luke 10:25–37; 1 Peter 4:8

POINTS TO PONDER–LOVE

A new commandment I give you: Love one another. As I have loved you, so you must love one another. By this all men will know that you are my disciples if you love one another.

JOHN 13:34–35

Love is not only something you feel. It's something you do.

DAVID WILKERSON

Joy is love exalted; peace is love in repose; long-suffering is love enduring; gentleness is love in society; goodness is love in action; faith is love on the battlefield; meekness is love in school; and temperance is love in training.

D. L. MOODY

I never knew how to worship until I knew how to love.

HENRY WARD BEECHER

We are shaped and fashioned by what we love.

GOETHE

Love is not blind—it sees more, not less. But because it sees more, it is willing to see less.

RABBI JULIUS GORDON

There is a land of the living and a land of the dead and the bridge is love, the only survival, the only meaning.

THORNTON WILDER

Tell me how much you know of the sufferings of your fellow men and I will tell you how much you have loved them.

HELMUT THIELICKE

The rule for all of us is perfectly simple. Do not waste time bothering whether you "love" your neighbor; act as if you did. As soon as we do this we find one of the great secrets. When you are behaving as if you loved someone, you will presently come to love him. If you injure someone you dislike, you will find yourself disliking him more. If you do him a good turn, you will find yourself disliking him less.

C. S. LEWIS

It is better to have loved and lost, than not to have loved at all.

ALFRED, LORD TENNYSON

All mankind loves a lover.

RALPH WALDO EMERSON

Love must be learned and learned again and again; there is no end to it. Hate needs no instruction, but waits only to be provoked.

KATHERINE ANNE PORTER

Our Lord does not care so much for the importance of our works as for the love with which they are done.

TERESA OF AVILA

The waste of life lies in the love we have not given, the powers we have not used, the selfish prudence which will risk nothing and which, shirking pain, misses happiness as well.

UNKNOWN

He that falls in love with himself will have no rivals.

BENJAMIN FRANKLIN

See also: Matthew 5:43–44; 1 Corinthians 13; 1 Peter 4:8; 1 John 4:19

W

E

E

K

4

THE SIX-MILLION-DOLLAR MAN

I praise you because I am fearfully and wonder-fully made.

PSALM 139:14

Everyone talks about the infinite preciousness of human beings, but one Yale University biochemist set out to prove it. Working with a chemistry supply company's catalog a few years ago, Harold J. Morowitz began tabulating the exact value of the human body.

At that point, hemoglobin ran $285 a gram; insulin, $47.50 a gram; human DNA, $76; collagen, $15; and alkaline phosphatase, $225, among others. On the more expensive side were such chemicals as bradykinin, which sold for $12,000 per gram; follicle-stimulating hormone, $8 million a gram, and prolactin, the hormone that stimulates female milk production, $17.5 million per gram.

When the price list was completed, Morowitz calculated how much of each chemical was in the human body and came up with an average value per gram of human body at $245.54. Multiplying that by his dry weight (68 percent of the body is water), he tallied his final value: $6,000,015.44.

Our test-tube value reflects the fact that God splurged on his Human Project. He could have kept things simple, as he did with his Tree or Rock Project. But he chose to make us more lavish, a fact mirrored in everything from our hearts (an "engine" that typically runs without rest or repair for 70+ years) to something as extravagantly ordinary as our skin. (This self-healing outer sheathing is tough and resilient, yet responds to minute changes in temperature, and reacts like Fourth of July sparklers when stroked by one's love.)

My problem is that I'm generally not aware of my six-million-dollar body. Sure, I notice it when I'm clogged with a cold. Or when I get BO. But then I just swallow some colored pills, or switch deodorants . . . and forget about me.

A unique, miraculous creation of God? Oh, I suppose. But on a day-to-day basis, I'm more awestruck by the apparent miracles of architects and engineers who build skyscrapers and space shuttles. When I look in the mirror each morning, I don't think, "Wow, God, thanks for splurging on my body!" Instead I think, "If I could just get rid of the zit on my nose ..."

And if God were to open the door for body alterations, I'd elbow my way to the front of the line.

See also: Genesis 1:26–31; Matthew 6:25–34; 1 Corinthians 6:19–20

COURAGE TO CONTINUE

Be strong and courageous. Do not be terrified; do not be discouraged, for the Lord your God will be with you wherever you go.

JOSHUA 1:9

The story of Kathy Miller didn't begin the day she was born. It really started the March afternoon she darted across the four-lane highway near her home in Scottsdale, Arizona. One of the drivers hit his brakes to avoid her. The car skidded. There was a scream. Many thought Kathy Miller was dead.

The report from hospital neurosurgeons was grim. She not only had compound fractures of one leg, but severe brain injuries as well. She lapsed into a coma–like a deep sleep from which she would never awaken. Days stretched into weeks with no sign of improvement. She dwindled from 110 to 55 pounds. It wasn't until late May that she could open her eyes. Even that was a miracle.

When she was finally released in June to go home, she couldn't talk or walk. She wore diapers and acted like an infant. She could barely even grunt out the word *Mama*. But Kathy had a strange idea. She wanted to run. Not just walk, but run–and run in a mini-marathon. She trusted God for courage to try.

Long, agonizing months passed as Kathy tried to regain coordination. She would shuffle a few steps, then catch hold of a wall or door. The first time she tried to jog a few steps she fell flat on her face, fracturing her nose. But she got up and kept trying, day after day. She fell again and again. But she kept getting up, determined to regain coordination.

And then on a crisp November day, eight months after her accident, Kathy entered the 10,000-meter North Bank Run in Phoenix. She didn't come close to finishing first. In fact, the thousands of other runners were far ahead by the time she'd managed to go a block. But she won *her* race, because she finished. She went the distance.

When failure or unfortunate incidents occur in your life, you have a choice. You can shake your fist and blame God—that is, you can *give up*. Or, you can *grow up*—you can trust God to help you fight off the discouragements and, like Kathy, take that one step at a time to regain your footing.

When down times come, remember that you are not alone: "For the LORD your God will be with you wherever you go." That encouragement is echoed in Isaiah 40:30–31: "Even youths grow tired and weary, and young men stumble and fall; but *those who hope in the LORD* will renew their strength. They will soar on wings like eagles; they will run and not grow weary, they will walk and not be faint."

So, best wishes. Not for your future success, but for your future misfortune. And may these adverse times be extravagant and enormously, outrageously joyful—for it's at these very moments Christ's strength moves in on your weakness. It's his way of helping you grow up.

See also: 2 Corinthians 12:9; Hebrews 12:1–11; James 1:2–4

STRANDED

> *God is our refuge and strength, an ever-present help in trouble.*

> **PSALM 46:1**

I was in an unfamiliar city, and it was starting to snow as I pulled onto the expressway. Merging into the rush of late-night traffic, my engine suddenly lost power. I pulled over in a panic. I was stranded in sub-zero weather, stuck in a section where the road curved drunkenly toward the sleazy downtown district. I waited for someone to stop, but no one did. They'd read too many newspaper stories.

I felt as insignificant as a piece of discarded roadside litter as I waited in the shadow of the lonely city on that black, snowy night. I was scared; I was cold. So I did the only thing I could think of: I told God I needed help. I asked him to ease my anxieties, and thanked him that he knew exactly where I was.

As cars hurtled past, I realized I had no choice but to trust God. And in that moment I became aware that God was enough. I then tried to think of Bible verses I knew: *"Never will I leave you; never will I forsake you."* It was a promise of God's I could count on—regardless of what happened. *"The Lord is my helper; I will not be afraid."* It was an assurance God could be trusted—regardless of the outcome.

At that moment, a sense of God's peace overwhelmed me. Praying to him was like talking with a best friend. And a few minutes later a sort of miracle happened. A car pulled over to help.

It's often true that when I dwell on myself and my problems, my troubles seem to grow. But when I dwell on God, my troubles seem to go. That doesn't mean things are always bright and rosy. Christians aren't immune to hurt and heartache. Yet God gives us a special capacity to cope with such times.

Chet Bitterman, a young missionary slain by Colombian terrorists, was probably praying for God's help up until the moment a bullet entered his head. God may have *seemingly* not been there. But he is *always* there. It's just that for a reason only God knows, he sometimes chooses not to intervene directly in human affairs. He saved Daniel in the lion's den. But he didn't save Christ on the cross. Does that mean God was dozing or negligent? No. He had other plans.

In my case I was saved. I was rescued. I know that others sometimes are not. Christians die every day. Yet even at that moment of death, Christ is there—offering a harbor in heaven for the storm-tossed vessel. And even there—yes, especially there—God is our refuge and our strength.

See also: Psalm 23; Hebrews 13:5–6; Revelation 21:4

THE QUITTING COMPLEX

See to it that you complete the work you have received in the Lord.

COLOSSIANS 4:17

Tom had big dreams for a quitter. His problem was he never stuck with anything past the dream stage.

He had the voice to become another Michael W. Smith and talked about how he'd cut an album by his twenty-first birthday. But when he quit his band over a dispute with another member, he never much mentioned music anymore. Instead, Tom said he'd run for the city council after graduation as the "youngest-ever" representative. But that dream was aborted when he couldn't even get elected class treasurer his senior year.

In view of his past, I was a bit cynical when Tom became a Christian. I figured it would be just like everything else in his life.

And it was. A couple of months later he "gave up on God" and started turning up stoned at football games.

"The Christian thing just didn't work out," Tom said when I asked him about it. "I'm tired of being all goody-goody. You know, playing Mister Nice Guy all of the time."

Tom was not some strange, abnormal, butterfly-type person who always flits from one thing to another. Sure, he quit a lot. But probably no more than you or I do, if we're counting. We all have dreams and goals that we don't follow through on. And if we don't actually "quit" being Christians, we're all pretty good at dragging our feet.

I sometimes feel a lot like Tom—that I'm just playacting as a Christian and pretending I'm nice and good and loving, when I know inside I'm not that way at all. The Russian writer Turgenev said it best when he wrote, "I don't know what the heart of a bad man is like, but I do know what the heart of a good man is like—and it's terrible."

I think the writers of the Bible knew the same feelings at times. That's why, in talking about the Christian faith, they use hard words like *struggle*, *race*, *battle*. Paul says we should "work out" our battle with sin daily. He knew what he was talking about: the battle against sin is just that, a bloody, never-ending battle. It's not easy to be a Christian in a non-Christian world. Even faith is not easy. When Christ said your faith could move mountains, he didn't mean it was as simple as saying "Presto-chango!" He meant that faith that moves mountains always carries a pick.

See also: Galatians 5:7; Philippians 2:12

IT IS FINISHED!

I press on toward the goal to win the prize for which God has called me heavenward in Christ Jesus.

PHILIPPIANS 3:14

When Christ died on the cross, his last words were, "It is finished!" There was nothing he left undone. He met his every goal on earth.

That seems unusual today, because many people's goals are never realized. They either don't pursue them or ditch the effort partway through. These might be such everyday goals as perfecting a serve in tennis or eating fewer Twinkies and losing twenty pounds. Your goals could be to get straight A's and earn a college scholarship. Or they may focus on the spiritual areas of your life, such as quitting a bad habit or rededicating your life to God.

Take a few minutes and think about what's holding you back from starting to work on—and finishing—the goals you've set in your own life. Write your reasons below:

I haven't _____ because _____.

I haven't _____ because _____.

I haven't _____ because _____.

If you've never thought much about setting goals before, consider making some for each of the different areas of your life: social, physical, mental, *and* spiritual. And then post them where you'll see them daily, perhaps on your locker door. When tempted to waver, try letting God restimulate you to *keep on* instead of giving up. Read the verse above slowly. Paul was determined not to quit on God. He had his eye on the goal, where God is beckoning us onward—to Jesus. He was off and running, and wasn't about to turn back. (Read 2 Cor. 11:24–33 to better understand what this goal entailed for him.)

Now, rewrite the passage (Phil. 3:14) in your own words, relating it to your personal situations: _____

See also: 1 Corinthians 9:24–27

COVER-UP

When Mary reached the place where Jesus was and saw him, she fell at his feet and said, "Lord, if you had been here, my brother would not have died." When Jesus saw her weeping, and the Jews who had come along with her also weeping, he was deeply moved in spirit and troubled. "Where have you laid him?" he asked. "Come and see, Lord," they replied. Jesus wept.

JOHN 11:32–35

When I was a new Christian, I got the impression it was important not to be overly emotional. Other Christians I knew seemed to be always happy and controlled no matter what. If they did poorly on a test, they smiled and praised God. If a relative died, they smiled and praised God.

The message was clear: God has given Christians a special ability to cope with life. You know, Romans 8:28. And if you express deep, personal feelings such as grief, anger, or despair, well, it's obvious you're not behaving as a mature Christian should—that you've lost control and don't have enough faith.

So I tried to suppress my feelings when I learned a close friend had been operated on for cancer and wasn't expected to live another year. I fought to remain levelheaded, neutrally pleasant, and emotionally unexpressive—to act like I thought a good Christian should. But it was like trying to keep an inner tube under water. The suppressed feelings just resurfaced as tension, and I couldn't sleep nights.

I was surprised when I first read in the Bible how Jesus reacted when his good friend died. He didn't erupt with pious clichés about Lazarus being in heaven with God. He wept. And when he encountered money changers in the temple, he didn't politely ask them to pack their bags and set things up down the block. No, he chased them out and kicked their tables over.

Reading things like those, I realized if Jesus didn't flaunt an attitude of spiritual self-sufficiency, I shouldn't. If I always try to seem strong to others, who am I fooling? God created me with the capacity for strong, spontaneous emotions. And he can spot a cover-up a mile away.

See also: Mark 11:15–18; Luke 19:41; Romans 12:15

JUST ANOTHER SOMEBODY

Be gracious to me, for I am lonely.

PSALM 25:16

I sometimes wondered what it would be like to be student-body president, to look good in a swimsuit, to have people call my name and wave across the cafeteria, to have my picture in the school newspaper.

But that's just for other people, I figured. It would never happen to me.

I sat behind a cheerleader in geometry. She always had a ribbon in her hair—sometimes red, sometimes blue, sometimes yellow. It was always pressed and perfectly tied on a braid of her chocolate hair.

One day I saw her with her mom at the nearby mall. It was a Saturday, and I nearly bumped into her as I rounded the corner out of the music shop.

"Excuse me," I quickly muttered. When I looked up and saw it was her, I nearly died of embarrassment. But I forced a smile and said "Hi." She said "Hi" back, but in a real nonchalant way, then kept walking.

"Who was that?" I heard her mom say as they passed by.

"I don't know," the cheerleader said. "Just somebody from class."

Just somebody from class. That made me sound so anonymous, so faceless. I'd been sitting behind her the entire year, and she didn't even know my name. I knew hers ... even her middle name.

Why does school have to be such a lonely place, Lord? The question popped into my mind one day on a bus ride home from school. It was so crowded that there were two, sometimes three to a seat. Some freshman girl I didn't know was crammed beside me.

You'd think with all these kids, school would be one great party. Maybe it is for others, but not for me, I thought. *You know my name, don't you, Lord? I just wish you weren't the only one.*

I glanced at the girl next to me. On any other day, I probably would not have given her a second thought. But she looked as lonely as I felt. When our eyes unexpectedly met, I forced an awkward smile. I didn't know what to say, but I mumbled something that made her smile. She said something back, and I responded.

It was a brief exchange with somebody I didn't know, but in those moments I got out of my skin and didn't feel so lonely. I think it was the same for the girl, who probably got on the bus feeling like a sardine and left feeling like somebody noticed her.

That's when it struck me: the antidote for loneliness is to build bridges with other people instead of walls. That's not a particularly cosmic thought, I know. But it's something to remember on those blue, just-another-somebody days.

See also: Matthew 5:46–47; John 15:9–17; Revelation 21:1–4

WEEK

5

A BROAD PERSPECTIVE

You are familiar with all my ways.

PSALM 139:3

The stewardess is saying something about seat belts, but no one is listening. They're glancing at watches, reading magazines, peering about as if they expect their boss or worst teacher to walk down the aisle at any moment.

Like them, I am still recovering from the whirl of last-minute details, my race-car rush to the airport, my dodging, darting dash to gate 33. My nerves, strung tighter than Steinway strings, begin to loosen only when the plane hurtles skyward after a screaming, bounding sprint down the rubber-streaked runway.

I glance out the fishbowl window at the shrinking landscape and feel my concerns drop away with the houses, cars, and people below. Loosening my seat belt, I watch quietly as my hurricane-paced world disappears and then peekaboos through the lace cover of clouds. Lakes glisten like jewels on the patchwork quilt of countryside, now 36,000 feet below.

At moments like this, I sense God views my life like I view the world that spreads now from horizon to horizon. Not that he's tucked, snoozing, beneath a blanket of clouds, unconcerned with life below. No, he's *personally* concerned because he has sampled our anxieties, hurts, and loneliness. *He has lived as one of us.*

Because of that, he can view my life personally and totally. He sees the roads I roam—where I've been and where I'm headed. He sees the valleys I must travel through, the mountains I must cross, the lonely plains I must necessarily rove. He knows where the detours are. He knows everything because he has a broad perspective.

But God doesn't just watch—he *directs.* I'm not an ant swallowed up in the vastness of the planet. To him I'm a unique creation of his that he will lovingly and individually guide through every detour and over every hill. He knows whose paths will intersect my own, and when. Marriage? College? Career? God has it all planned.

People seek release from their pressures in many different ways. Some calm their nerves with a six-pack or shot of whiskey. A line of coke or a couple of pills might do it for others. And then there are those who seek release sexually.

For me, it's enough to periodically soar skyward, to rocket above my world and view life from a new perspective. God's perspective. It's a high that stays with me long after I am back on the ground.

See also: Psalm 23; Isaiah 42:16; 46:10; Matthew 6:25–34

WHAT WILL YOU DO?

> *"What shall I do, then, with Jesus who is called Christ?" Pilate asked. They all answered, "Crucify him!"*
>
> MATTHEW 27:22

Much of human communication is based on questions. Among the dozens you hear every day are: "What time do we eat?" "Where do you want to go Friday?" "When is the next home game?" and "Do you need a lift?"

More momentous questions include: "Will I get well?" "Can you raise my grade?" "Will you marry me?" and "Can I borrow the car?"

Some of the Bible's most notable passages are questions. The first recorded question occurred when the serpent in the Garden of Eden raised a doubt in Eve's mind by asking, "Did God *really* say, 'You must not eat from any tree in the garden'?"

Other key questions from Scripture include: "Will a man rob God?" "Who do people say the Son of Man is?" "What good thing must I do to get eternal life?" "My God, my God, why have you forsaken me?" and "What can a man give in exchange for his soul?"

But one of the Bible's most memorable questions came from the lips of Pontius Pilate, an up-and-coming politician who was sent by Roman authorities to be governor of Palestine. He was in his Jerusalem chambers one day when some hot-under-the-collar Jews stormed in, demanding the execution of Jesus, who was then but 33.

Pilate had heard about Christ—the miracles and the bizarre claims of being God's only son. News like that makes headlines. So he spent a few minutes questioning Jesus about these things and quickly determined that he had committed no capital offense. But Pilate didn't know what to do next. He couldn't just ignore Jesus. And because he was a politician, dependent on public opinion, he could hardly ignore the crowd either.

So he asked the masses, "What shall I do with Jesus who is called Christ?" Their predetermined response: "Crucify him!"

After some two thousand years, Pilate is remembered as the man who washed his hands of Christ by abandoning him to mob fury. That action, in itself, was a choice. Over the centuries, Pilate's question has also not been forgotten. It still rings today. You, too, must decide what you will do with Christ.

As Christians, we face that choice every day in how we respond to other people, circumstances, and temptation. You know Christ can't be ignored. But will you abandon him? Follow him? Recrucify him? You've got Christ on your hands. *What will you do with him?*

See also: Joshua 24:15; Matthew 16:13–16

▓ IT'S A MAD, MAD WORLD

Come to me, all you who are weary and burdened, and I will give you rest.

MATTHEW 11:28

From one day to the next, one year to the next, newspaper headlines and CNN broadcasts don't seem to change. Armies invade neighboring countries. Assassins topple governments. Earthquakes level major cities. Politicians steal the public blind. Something else causes cancer. Another rock idol ODs on drugs. And some lunatic is loose in public.

Things aren't much better at school. Fights break out almost daily. A major drug raid leads to seventeen student arrests, including my good friend. The homecoming queen gets pregnant. The football coach keels over with a heart attack. The Coke machine is busted into again. My girlfriend begins dating someone else. And I flunk an algebra test.

On the home front, some of my parents' best friends announce their pending divorce, my dad gets on me about mowing the lawn, and my mom never stops harping about my homework. My sister hogs the bathroom. My brother is his usual slob self. My aunt comes to stay on one day's notice. And I get laid off at work.

If you're anything like me, you sometimes feel overwhelmed by the chaos of life and people around you. There are days when nothing or no one makes sense, and you're convinced you're the last surviving sane person. On days when I feel like that, it helps me to tell God and get the burden off my shoulders. That doesn't mean things will change overnight . . . or necessarily at all. It just makes me feel better to know God understands how I feel.

In James 4:8 the Bible says, "Come near to God and he will come near to you." *The Message* puts it this way: "Say a quiet *yes* to God and he'll be there in no time." So take God up on the promise by talking to him on those days you feel as helpless as a wind-tossed rag. It's great relief to sense God's presence. He wants to be the still point of your turning, twisting, ever-changing world.

See also: Jeremiah 31:25; Matthew 24:4–33; John 7:37

WEIGHT LIFTER

If my people, who are called by my name, will humble themselves and pray and seek my face and turn from their wicked ways, then will I hear from heaven and will forgive their sin and will heal their land.

2 CHRONICLES 7:14

There are days when I feel that awful weight
    Dragging me, slowing me, nearly drowning me
As if I'm swimming with all my clothes on.
    With each stroke I grow more weary and think,
"If only I had a rock to cling to...."
    Such is the weight of unforgiven sin in my life.
And then I hear God's still small voice
    Whispering that he is that rock—
Able to greatly forgive because he greatly loves.
    "So you think you've really blown it?" the Lord kindly asks,
    "You think there's no hope for you this time?" he gently breathes.
And then he urges me to consider how:
David must have felt when he tried to hide
    His infidelity by killing his lover's husband;
Abram must have felt when he sacrificed
    His wife's chastity to save his own neck;
Peter must have felt when he denied
    That he'd ever known or followed Christ;
Sarah must have felt when she laughed
    At God for making a promise she thought he couldn't keep;
Esau must have felt when he traded
    His birthright for a hot bowl of chili;
Rahab must have felt when she flopped

Into bed after bed after bed, playing the prostitute;
And the list goes on and on and on . . .
But God graciously allows people new beginnings
When they realize they need help—and a rock to cling to.
Be that rock, dear Lord, for me today.

See also: 1 John 1:5–10; 2:1–6

THE SEX TRAP

Flee from sexual immorality. All other sins a man commits are outside his body, but he who sins sexually sins against his own body. Do you not know that your body is a temple of the Holy Spirit, who is in you, whom you have received from God?

1 CORINTHIANS 6:18–19

I had dated Sandy nearly a year when she broke up with me and started going out with Dave. It hurt to see her with someone else, but I felt crushed when I learned they were having sex.

When we were going together, Sandy always talked about how God was No. 1 in her life. We were active in church, and there was never any question about her stand on sex. She knew the Bible said it was wrong outside of marriage.

I lost track of her when I went away to college . . . until a mutual friend said he'd heard Sandy had gotten pregnant and had a baby. Then one day I was home on break and bumped into her in the post office. Her little boy was screaming. I didn't really know what to say, so I mumbled something about her kid having a good set of lungs. She laughed. Then I asked about Dave.

"We broke up shortly after I got pregnant," she said, nodding at her toddler. "Dave didn't want the responsibility. So I've got it all." She forced a smile, then shook her head. "You know, I never thought it would be this way. When Dave was still around, I felt like such a hypocrite. I guess that's why I dropped out of church. It was easier not thinking about God. But I got things straightened out with God when Jason was born, and I'm going to church again."

I was glad to know she was doing better spiritually. Yet it was still sad to hear the tone of regret in her voice. I realized as I stood there that while God's forgiveness relieves the guilt, it doesn't always erase the consequences of sin. Sandy's trying to raise little Jason alone was proof of that.

See also: Romans 6:11–23; Galatians 6:7–10

FAULT FINDERS

> *He who conceals his sins does not prosper, but whoever confesses and renounces them finds mercy.*
>
> **PROVERBS 28:13**

Whenever Judy blew it, she always blamed others. When I picked her up for a date and had to wait thirty minutes, she never even said she was sorry.

"My brother hogged the shower," was the best she could do.

In a history class we shared, she never accepted the responsibility for her low grades. Whenever she botched a test, it was because "I can't *believe* the picky details that dumb teacher expects us to know!" Or "None of this stuff is important anyway. Who cares about ancient history two hundred years ago." Or "I really tried to study for this one, but my parents' gabby friends stopped by."

It was the same in other areas of her life. When she forgot to add chocolate chips to the cookie dough, it was because I had distracted her. And one day when she ran out of gas and was late for work, she blamed her dad for not filling the tank the day before. Finally I lost my patience with her.

"No matter what happens, it's always someone else's fault," I said. "Are you perfect or something? Have you ever told anyone you were sorry?"

When I thought about Judy after we'd broken up, I realized the basic difference between us was simply that she verbalized the kinds of excuses I often just mumbled silently to myself. *"I was blinded by the sun,"* I'd think when I fumbled an easy pass reception in PE. *"If that jerk only knew how to drive!"* I'd quietly curse when the driver I was tailgating braked suddenly. I always had ways to explain away my mistakes.

I have a tendency to want to do the same with sin. I can blame away sin, I can ignore sin, I can conceal sin—all in an effort to look good to God. Trouble is, God sees through our shallow cover-ups. Before him, we're as guilty as the worst criminal. We've all been caught. But he has promised to forgive us and erase our record if we "come clean" and confess our sin. That's the key. The only way to look good before God is to admit our absolute worst.

See also: Isaiah 1:18; 1 John 1:8–10

POINTS TO PONDER—SIN

For the wages of sin is death, but the gift of God is eternal life in Christ Jesus our Lord.

ROMANS 6:23

Even in this age of inflation, the wages of sin remain the same.

ANONYMOUS

There are only two kinds of people: the righteous who believe themselves sinners, and the rest, sinners who believe themselves righteous.

BLAISE PASCAL

Hate the sin, but love the sinner.

THOMAS BUCHANAN READ

Christians who get involved in sin are miserable. They've closed the door on sin and then spend their lives looking through the keyhole.

JAY KESLER

As Chesterton pointed out, the Fall of Man is only the banana-skin joke carried to cosmic proportions.

MALCOLM MUGGERIDGE

Adam ate the apple, and our teeth still ache.

HUNGARIAN PROVERB

People are not punished for their sins, but by them.

ELBERT HUBBARD

The sins of the flesh are bad, but they are the least bad of all sins. All the worst pleasures are purely spiritual: the pleasure of putting other people in the wrong, of bossing and patronizing and spoiling sport, and back-biting; the pleasures of power, of hatred.... That is why a cold, self-righteous prig who goes regularly to church may be far nearer to hell than a prostitute. But, of course, it is better to be neither.

C. S. LEWIS

One reason sin flourishes is that it is treated like a cream puff instead of a rattlesnake.

BILLY SUNDAY

Man calls it an accident; God calls it an abomination. Man calls it a blunder; God calls it a blindness. Man calls it a defect; God calls it a disease. Man calls it a chance; God calls it a choice. Man calls it an error; God calls it an enmity. Man calls it a fascination; God calls it a fatality. Man calls it an infirmity; God calls it an iniquity.

Man calls it a luxury; God calls it a leprosy. Man calls it a liberty; God calls it lawlessness. Man calls it a trifle; God calls it a tragedy. Man calls it a mistake; God calls it a madness. Man calls it a weakness; God calls it willfulness.

MOODY MONTHLY

The sin they do by two and two they must pay for one by one.

RUDYARD KIPLING

My sins don't make me a sinner. They're just the evidence.

S. RICKLY CHRISTIAN

Sin is energy in the wrong channel.

AUGUSTINE OF HIPPO

Sin may be clasped so close we cannot see its face.

RICHARD CHENEVIX TRENCH

We shall never understand anything of our Lord's preaching and ministry unless we continually keep in mind what exactly and exclusively his errand was in this world. Sin was his errand in this world, and it was his only errand. He would never have been in this world, either preaching or doing anything else but for sin. He could have done everything else for us without coming down into this world at all; everything else but take away our sin.

ALEXANDER WHYTE

See also: Psalm 51:1–17; Isaiah 1:18; Matthew 9:10–12; Romans 8:1–14

WEEK 6

CONTAGIOUS OR CONTAMINATED?

"God's name is blasphemed ... because of you."

ROMANS 2:24

Tom grew disenchanted with Christianity when he took a hard look at Christians around him. His Bible study leader was having an affair with a married woman. Another Christian leader he trusted had refused to sell his house to a couple ... just because they were black. One of the regulars at church, the mother of his friend, practically had an IV hooked up to a gin bottle.

"If *they* call themselves Christians," he said, "count me out."

Hypocrisy has been a stumbling block for non-Christians since the days of the early church. In writing to the Roman church about Jews, Paul turned on the heat. He charged that their belief had turned to legalism and their commitment to God had become a "form of religion." Sure, they seemed good enough in their own eyes. They prayed and read Scripture. They tithed their money, fasted, and attended their churches and synagogues often enough to be labeled "active" and "faithful." But something was drastically wrong. They knew *what* they believed, but none of it affected their day-to-day living.

"You who teach others, do you not teach yourselves?" Paul wrote. "You who preach against stealing, do you steal? You who say that people should not commit adultery, do you commit adultery? You who abhor idols, do you rob temples? You who brag about the law, do you dishonor God by breaking the law?" (Rom. 2:21–23).

Yes to all of the above. The result: their "churchianity" and "religiosity" had turned people away from the Lord. "God's name is blasphemed because of you!" Paul blasted.

In a letter sent to the Corinthians, Paul describes Christians as "Christ's ambassadors." He also notes that God has "committed to us the message of reconciliation." In other words, God uses Christians to reach nonbelievers. We are his mouthpiece, his arms, his means of conveying love. And when that message is corrupted by our actions, others notice. They see through the phoniness of religion.

The easy solution is just to warn people that Christians are human and fallible—and urge them to judge God only by himself. That's true, of course. But the fact is, God has established us as his representatives. And if our Christianity isn't contagious, it very likely is contaminated.

See also: 2 Corinthians 5:17–21; James 1:22–25

THE BUCK STOPS HERE

It is more blessed to give than to receive.

ACTS 20:35

One day I became curious about where my money was disappearing. I didn't make much working part-time after school at the box company, so I wasn't exactly loaded. But I earned enough to know I shouldn't be constantly broke.

To solve the mystery, I got out my checkbook and started flipping back through all the little scribble notes I had made when I wrote each check: the data that tells me *when* and *where* I spent *how much* for *what.*

The Timberland boots ate a wad. And it was hard to believe I'd spent $136 on gas in one month. The amount I paid for new Michelin radials made me wince. But like I told Dad, the guys at school would laugh me off campus if I drove on Tijuana retreads. There was the day I bombed my history exam and got wasted on waffle cones at TCBY; the pair of Nikes (because I felt pig-guilty about TCBY); the $37 blown on a lousy date with that dumb sophomore; three new CDs and a new compact player to better enjoy them. The list became a blur of jots and figures as I flipped faster.

It's odd, but I'd always thought of myself as a caring person, one who was concerned about others. But the truth is, I was *most* concerned about myself. My checkbook proved it. Priorities are generally mirrored by how you spend your money. Is it always for yourself? Or do you consider how you can meet others' needs?

What are some of those needs? Well, I'd ignored several just in the previous month. I thought of the family that got burned out of their house and lost *everything*. Maybe I could have made them a meal or bought them a sack of burgers. I could have done something similar for the homeless guy on the corner who looked like he was starving. Instead I walked around him. A flower would have brightened the day of the elderly lady next door. Maybe I could have spent *my time*—just ten minutes to help Mom with the dishes, call my grandfather, or clean Dad's brush after he painted the living room. I had the time to go with our youth group to the orphan home, but I'd opted for the beach.

Sometimes it's hard to change selfish habits. But the task is made easier when I consider that everything I have is a gift from God. Freely I have received, so freely should I give.

See also: Matthew 25:31–46; Mark 12:41–44

HEART TREASURES

Where your treasure is, there your heart will be also.

MATTHEW 6:21

I was watching CNN when scenes of a Southern California fire flashed across the TV. The windswept inferno had destroyed million-dollar estates on its flaming rampage through the bushy hillsides of Los Angeles. A reporter interviewed a man who, hours earlier, had lost his home. He described how he'd only had a couple of minutes to grab a few belongings, stash them in his minivan, and escape with his life.

What would you do in a similar situation? You're awakened in the middle of the night by a sheriff's deputy who tells you to evacuate immediately—a fire is sweeping toward your home and will engulf it within minutes. You can salvage only 10 belongings. What would they be? Write down the first items that come to mind:

1. _____
2. _____
3. _____
4. _____
5. _____
6. _____
7. _____
8. _____
9. _____
10. _____

Now review the list. The Bible says the things you treasure reveal a lot about you and your values. What kinds of things did you value enough to risk your life retrieving? What did you grab first? Last? What did you leave behind? What does all this say about the values you live by?

See also: Colossians 3:1–3

HEMMED IN

You hem me in—behind and before; you have laid your hand upon me. Such knowledge is too wonderful for me, too lofty for me to attain.

PSALM 139:5–6

79

There is generally nothing positive about being "hemmed in." The term makes you think of those hot-tempered, "GET-OFF-MY-BACK!" confrontations with your parents or those high-decibel, "GET-OUT-OF-MY-ROOM!" face-offs with your kid brother. Being "hemmed in" is a claustrophobic, itchy, cornered kind of feeling that usually makes you want to slam the door and crank up the stereo.

But when David uses the phrase pertaining to God, he doesn't shake his fist and scream skyward. Instead he gets real gushy and says, in effect, "I see you, God, everywhere I look: before me, behind me, and right next to me. I'm amazed—that's almost too wonderful to believe!" Why isn't David threatened? Because God's closeness isn't meant to be stifling.

God stands behind you. David's words, "You hem me in—behind," are similar to Isaiah's: "God . . . will be your rear guard." This is army talk. It refers to the group of soldiers that follow the main regiment, helping stragglers and more or less picking up the pieces. God is that way—he follows behind, mending and restoring your hurts and sorrows. He forgives your sin and helps you back on your feet. He picks up the pieces of your life, creating positive results from negative incidents.

God stands before you. We don't know what challenges we'll face next week, next month, next year. We don't know where our future leads. But God does, because he's scouted up ahead. "The LORD himself goes before you," says Moses in Deuteronomy. It's a promise you can count on.

God stands with you. As David writes here, "You have laid your hand upon me." It's his way of saying God doesn't just stand back and watch from a distance the goings-on in your life. He's at your side, encouraging and challenging—helping you through the rough times and celebrating with you during the high times.

Yes, you are hemmed in by God. But like David, you can be hemmed in . . . and happy!

See also: Deuteronomy 31:8; Isaiah 52:12; Jeremiah 29:11

THOSE WERE THE DAYS

As God's chosen people, holy and dearly loved, clothe yourselves with compassion, kindness, humility, gentleness and patience. Bear with each other and forgive whatever grievances you may have against one another. Forgive as the Lord forgave you. And over all these virtues put on love, which binds them all together in perfect unity. Let the peace of Christ rule in your hearts, since as members of one body you were called to peace. And be thankful.

COLOSSIANS 3:12–15

On a shelf in my closet is a stack of school yearbooks going back to junior high. My parents didn't shoot videos, so the yearbooks are the only record of who I was and what I was like back then. They contain those years in pictures: the candid moments, the formal try-and-look-studly shots, the best of times, the worst of times.

What the school photographer couldn't or didn't capture, my friends often did. They scribbled comments in the margins about the times we shared: "Remember when . . ." or "I'll never forget the time when . . ." Some said things like, "I wish we could have gotten to know each other better, but . . ."

Reviewing old yearbooks is sort of like entering a time warp. You aren't the same person you were back then. Times have changed. And you have, too.

Take a slug of nostalgia sometime today and dig out your yearbooks. Read what people wrote about you. What adjectives surface most frequently in their descriptions of you? Nice? Bodacious? Crazy? Party animal? Quiet? Brainy? Driven? Funny?

As you flip through the pages, keep track of the descriptions that surface most frequently. Are any of the adjectives like those Paul

81

used in the verse above to describe Christians: compassionate, kind, humble, forgiving, loving, thankful?

Christ said each of us is to be a light to our own corner of the world. You should be the bright spot in people's lives. If you truly are, you'll read about it in your yearbooks.

See also: Matthew 5:13–16; 28:18–20; Galatians 5:22–25

THE MULTIPLICATION FACTOR

As evening approached, the disciples came to him and said, "This is a remote place, and it's already getting late. Send the crowds away, so they can go to the villages and buy themselves some food." Jesus replied, "They do not need to go away. You give them something to eat."

MATTHEW 14:15–16

When this bit of dialogue took place, dusk was settling over the Sea of Galilee. The thousands of people tagging along after Jesus were hungry, and there was no McDonald's nearby. The disciples could hear the thousands of children begging to go home to eat. So they urged Christ to adjourn the waterfront meeting. Their solution was to let the people fend for themselves: "Send the crowds away!"

But Jesus shook his head. "They do not need to go away," he said. "*You* give them something to eat."

I imagine some of the twelve disciples glanced at each other and rolled their eyes. It had been a long, hot day. *Sure, Jesus,* Peter may have giggled at Christ's seemingly absurd suggestion. There simply was nothing to eat—nothing, that is, except a sack lunch donated to the cause by a kid who undoubtedly had overheard Christ talking with the disciples.

The child didn't have much—just a few pieces of bread and some fish—but he gave what he had. One of the disciples, Andrew,

82

counted the bread and fish, then shrugged. "Here is a boy with five small barley loaves and two small fish, but how far will they go among so many?" The question was not unreasonable. But Andrew forgot he was talking to Christ, who once declared: "I am the bread of life. He who comes to me will never go hungry."

Each day we face similar situations. Christ has asked of us the apparently impossible: to be his ambassadors in a dying world; to be his witnesses at home, at work, at school; to *give people something to eat.*

That entails things like reaching outside of your clique for friends, being more open about sharing your faith, setting a positive example by not gossiping or lying. In other words, it means *living* the gospel—*being* the "Good News." We can analyze the odds against us, and shrug off the task because of our limited talent, time, and money. Like Andrew, we can focus on our *insufficiency.*

Or, like the young boy, we can focus on Christ's *sufficiency.* When we give Christ what little we have, he will take it and multiply it. The result now, as then, will be abundantly beyond what anyone can ask or dare think.

See also: Matthew 19:26; Mark 1:17; John 6:35

LOOKING FOR CHANGE

O Lord, you have searched me and you know me.
You know when I sit and when I rise; you perceive my
thoughts from afar. You discern my going out and my
lying down; you are familiar with all my ways.

PSALM 139:1–3

By the time I graduated from high school and completed two years of college, I was ready for a change. I wanted to get away from old friends, my family, from textbooks and Friday nights at the library, from the same old nickel-and-dime striving to get better grades. And I was bored with myself. So I went to Europe for a year. I thought that would solve all my problems.

At first, boredom didn't exist. New friends seemed more interesting than the old. They skied the Alps and spoke three languages. And there was always something different to do: restaurants and theaters and beaches I'd never been to before. It was exciting not knowing my way around—unlike back home where I had the city map memorized. Even getting lost was fun. And if I got the least bit bored with one city or tired of one beach, I hopped the next train to a new destination and started all over again.

Europe was everything travel posters said it would be, but after three months that wasn't enough. I got tired of living out of my backpack and hopping trains every few days. Soon I was as lonely and bored as I'd ever been at home. I actually got tired of all of the variety and newness. I longed for what I knew: home.

During that time, I began to realize I couldn't escape my problems. Sure, I could change my geography. I could change my hotel or hostel. I could change my friends, my school, my church, my wardrobe, my hairstyle. But none of that did much good because I was still stuck with myself.

My predicament was like the standard plot from an old sci-fi thriller: You see the monster and flee down the alley, duck into an open doorway, and double-bolt the door. Then you hear a noise and spin around, only to find you've locked yourself in with the monster. The monster, you see, is yourself.

When I've tried to change myself, I've gone about it wrong. In a sense, I'm much like a woman who has cosmetic surgery. A tuck here and an implant there will make her look different in the mirror, but inside she's still the same person. That's why God doesn't focus on externals. The surgery he conducts to make us more like him is done from the inside out—he starts with the heart, the monster's cage.

As I allow God to tame the monster within, that's when true change occurs; that's when I can begin living an abundant, forgiven, fulfilling life.

See also: Ezekiel 11:19; 2 Corinthians 5:17

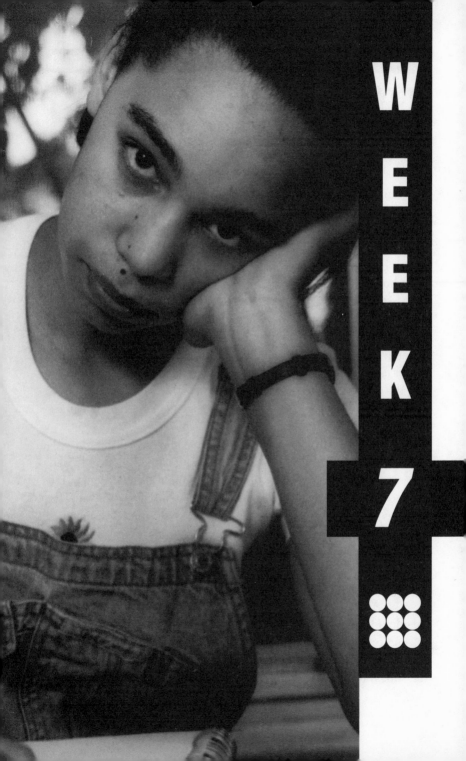

WEEK

7

DOWN, BUT NOT OUT

Be still, and know that I am God.

PSALM 46:10

Sometimes adults act as if stress affects only men and women who juggle jobs and kids and mortgages. They forget what it feels like to wander from classroom to classroom with your guts in a knot and your nerves stretched tighter than violin strings.

Stress: Your teacher calls on you for an answer you don't know. Heads turn, eyes wait. Your skin flushes and suddenly you feel very hot and very dumb.

Stress: You've been trying to get the courage to ask the new girl out. Will she even know who you are? Your hands go clammy as you dial her number. The phone rings and someone—must be her mother—answers. "Is Diane there?" you ask. "Yes, could I tell her who's calling?" the voice says. "Uh, no ... I mean, I think I've—like—got the wrong number," you blurt as you suddenly hang up.

Stress: Classmates treat you like a leper since you became a Christian. Even your best friend ignores you.

Stress: After twenty-two years of marriage, your parents announce they no longer love each other and are filing for divorce.

Stress: Your team could tie the game with a field goal, but the coach wants to gamble on fourth down and go for the win. He decides on a run and fingers you to carry the ball. You take the hand-off and slam straight ahead. A helmet smashes into your ribs and the ball pops loose. "FUMBLE: NUMBER 26," the loudspeakers boom. The stands erupt with a low-pitched razz of boos, and humiliation grips you like a coronary.

You try to pretend these things don't matter, but that ache inside tells you they *do.* Your mind taunts you with slow-motion, instant replays, eroding your self-confidence with each showing. You can bite your nails to the knuckle, but if you'd force yourself to stop, be still, and get reoriented, you'd discover God is close at hand.

That's what Psalm 46:1 is all about: God offers instant help when you face the big squeeze of stress and heartache. The ultimate security is knowing he is there . . . and always will be. He's given his spirit to guide, strengthen, and help you respond to whatever comes up, because you're part of his family. And as a member of it, you also have other Christian brothers and sisters to support you.

"I am God," the last three words in the verse say. That gives you certain bragging rights—the right to say, "I am God's child."

Stop what you're doing right now. No matter what is going on around you or inside you, put it all out of your mind. Clear your head. Pause a moment and blurt it out: *"I am God's child."*

Say it again, this time with an exclamation point.

Try it different ways: *"I* am God's child!" "I am *God's* child!" "I am God's *child!"* And smile when you say it.

You're not just another somebody on the treadmill of life. You're not a street orphan. You're *somebody.* You have the benefit of a rich and royal heritage, of being linked directly to the King of kings.

Knowing that, there's one thing you need to do. You need to start living like it.

See also: Matthew 11:28–30; John 14:27; 1 Thessalonians 5:10–11

THE SINGLE LIFE

I would like you to be free from concern. An unmarried man is concerned about the Lord's affairs—how he can please the Lord. But a married man is concerned about the affairs of this world—how he can please his wife—and his interests are divided. An unmarried woman or virgin is concerned about the Lord's affairs: Her aim is to be devoted to the Lord in both body and spirit. But a married woman is concerned about the affairs of this world—how she can please her husband.

1 CORINTHIANS 7:32–34

I am married. Many of my friends are married. And most of my friends who aren't, want to be. One of these single friends feels very bad that Mr. Right has yet to cross her path. When she didn't marry within a reasonable amount of time after graduation, she began to wonder what was wrong with her. Unfortunately, she views singleness like a disease. And every time she attends a wedding, she feels a little discarded, hurt, and bitter. She thinks God owes her a husband . . . and has never considered that he could have other, better plans for her life.

In contrast, I have another friend who developed such a love relationship with God that he has purposely not married. He knows how much time and energy marriage demands. He knows the personal and financial matters he'd face with a wife and kids. So he chose not to split his loyalty and love to God. Today, his "family" consists of hundreds of orphans living in the shantytowns of Mexico. Having quit his job and sold his possessions, he's free from outside concerns and has dedicated his entire life to serving these young poor—in a way that no married man or woman could.

The institution of marriage began when God created Eve for Adam. "It is not good for the man to be alone," God said. That's not the case for *every* man or woman—singleness is just the thing for some. Christ (a bachelor) indicated that some people are specifically called to the single life, and "have renounced marriage because of the kingdom of heaven" (Matt. 19:12). Paul (also a bachelor) later wrote, "It is good for a man not to marry" (1 Cor. 7:1).

They wanted people to know that marriage is an *option*—it's not for everyone—and that there are some very good things awaiting those who pursue God's calling to the single life.

See also: 1 Corinthians 7:8–9, 26–31

DEAR DIARY ...

Let the word of Christ dwell in you richly as you ...
sing psalms, hymns and spiritual songs with gratitude in
your hearts to God.

COLOSSIANS 3:16

Some people keep daily journals or diaries in which they chart their innermost thoughts and feelings. My sister had one. It was pink and flowery, with a little gold lock. She thought she had the only key. She did. But I had a paper clip that worked just as well.

In the Bible, many of the psalms are so personal that reading them feels as if you were snooping in someone's diary. Take Psalm 51, for example. Written by King David, it records his deepest sorrows after he had an affair with a neighbor and then killed her husband. Other psalms are just as autobiographical and personal.

Try your hand at writing a psalm, patterned after those in the Bible. Keep it as personal as a diary. When finished, rewrite the words on a 3 x 5 card and tape it in your Bible as Psalm 151.

O Lord, you know me inside out.
　When I feel _____
　Or think _____
Even then I know you will understand.

My future is laid bare before you.
　You know my concerns about _____
　And how I worry about _____
But I know I can trust you to guide me.

I give thanks to you, O Lord,
　Even though _____

And even when _____
Because I know you are in control, no matter what.

You are the stronghold of my life.
*   I shall not fear _____*
*   Or concern myself with _____*
For you will hold me, protect me, and comfort me
All the days of my life.

See also: Psalm 33:3; Ephesians 5:19; James 5:13

JUST LIKE YOU

> **The Lord your God goes with you; he will never
> leave you nor forsake you.**

DEUTERONOMY 31:6

There was a time when Paula knew her father. It was back
when she was about twelve. He seemed like the perfect father: he
coached her softball team, took the family on long vacations, and
kissed her mother each day before leaving for work.

But he changed over the years. He sometimes didn't come
home at night. And each week there seemed to be more empty
booze bottles in the trash. She didn't know what caused the changed
behavior; all she knew was that he'd become unrecognizable as the
father she once knew and trusted.

Then, a month before she left for college, she watched as he
loaded his belongings into a U-Haul trailer and left to start a new life
with his secretary, who was barely older than Paula herself. He
seemed like a forty-one-year-old fool, she thought, and then burst
into tears. She'd always looked to her father for guidance in the past.
Whatever he did was right . . . if only because he was grown up. But
as she discovered, there is no such thing as a grown-up person.

It's a dramatic moment when you first discover your parents have major character flaws and failings. Perhaps it hit you when your mom or dad, tired from a long day, lashed out at you with uncharacteristic anger. You might have done nothing to provoke them, aside from being in the same room at the wrong time. Yet they bombarded you with hurtful, howitzer words.

There are days when you probably feel more shocked than angry at their behavior. But you really shouldn't be too surprised, because the Bible says that such actions are what mark us as people. "*All* have sinned and fall short of the glory of God" leaves no one out, including parents. So if you expect them (or anyone else, for that matter) *not* to let you down, you can expect to be disappointed.

People never act like you want them to. Teachers and bosses can be unfair and overly demanding. Family members can be rude and selfish. Even friends can be biting and cruel. But then, you have your failings, too. Like your parents, you are not immune from that "mark of humanity." You, too, respond to others in hurtful, negative ways.

At such times, God doesn't hold a grudge or twist your arm until you act better. He simply waits for you to realize your sin, and then he wipes it from his memory. And he expects the same of us. As Christ said, "If you have anything against someone, *forgive* — only then will your heavenly Father be inclined to also wipe your slate clean of sins" (Mark 11:25 *The Message*).

That means you must recognize that your parents aren't "grown up" or perfect. You need to accept them for who they are: people who are basically *just like you.*

See also: Mark 11:25; Romans 3:23

THE BIG KAHUNA

You know that those who are regarded as rulers of the Gentiles lord it over them, and their high officials exercise authority over them. Not so with you. Instead, whoever wants to become great among you must be your servant, and whoever wants to be first must be slave of all. For even the Son of Man did not come to be served, but to serve, and to give his life as a ransom for many.

MARK 10:42–45

I once had a boss who treated everyone like dirt. She barked orders louder than a Marine drill sergeant and screamed hysterically at the least provocation. "Do this!" "Do that!" She wanted no one to forget that she was the boss.

I was unlucky enough to report directly to her, and my office was just down the hall. So my head was on the chopping block daily. My only reprieve was when she left town.

One day when my boss was on a business trip, I entered her cavernous office and glanced around quickly to make sure no one else was nearby. Then I slipped into her big, comfortable chair, leaned back and propped my feet on her sprawling desk.

"Someday," I thought, "I'll be in charge. I'll say 'Jump!' and they'll jump."

This attitude of wanting to be in control is, I suppose, natural enough. We want to be the Big Kahuna and give orders rather than take them. We want to be honored and esteemed. We'd like strangers to know our name and recognize us on the street. We tire of being pawns on someone else's chessboard, and would like to wield a little power ourselves for a change.

The Bible, however, has quite a different emphasis. "Whoever wants to become great among you must be your servant," said Christ, adding that he himself vacated heaven not to be a ruler of the masses, but to be a servant of many. He daily demonstrated this when he befriended the sick, the poor, the homeless. He washed a lot of feet. He demonstrated his Lordship by *not* lording.

"In humility consider others better than yourselves," Paul writes to the Philippians, adding: "Your attitude should be the same as that of Christ Jesus." The rub is that we are followers of a man whose attitude didn't get him crowned. It got him killed.

See also: Matthew 25:31–46; Philippians 2:1–11

CLEARING THE ROADS

Bear with each other and forgive whatever grievances you may have against one another. Forgive as the Lord forgave you.

COLOSSIANS 3:13

What starts as a light snow of lace-like flakes suddenly turns to a blizzard. What seems beautiful—a backdrop for a picture-perfect postcard—suddenly rages. Driving snow slashes with an arctic wind, obscuring vision and deepening drifts.

School loudspeakers blare: classes are immediately dismissed. You bundle up and trudge to your car as others scramble for the bus. You arrive home just as the streets become impassable and the city shuts down.

Eventually the snowplows come, heaving great plumes of snow skyward, pushing the snow back to once again allow traffic through. The barrier is removed. A city once paralyzed becomes a city revived.

When we hold grudges—refusing to forgive *and* forget—we block the communication between ourselves and God. Drifts of unfeeling concern pile up inside of us, chilling our hearts. But forgiveness is like the snowplow—once again opening the roadway. It sweeps the barriers aside and allows communication to be restored.

The Bible tells us to forgive whatever grievances we have ... as the Lord forgave us. His forgiveness of us is often linked to our forgiveness of others. "But you don't know the hurt I've faced," you charge. "I was knifed in the back by someone I thought was my friend. Forgive? You've got to be crazy! Forget? Never!"

Such thoughts were probably not far from Peter's mind when he came to Jesus and asked, "Lord, how many times shall I forgive my brother when he sins against me?" He mentally ran down the list of wrongs others had done him. "Up to seven times?" he probed, probably hoping that Jesus would say, "Don't be silly—you've got rights, too. Let others do you in two, maybe three times at most . . . and then get them back. "But Jesus actually answered, "I tell you, not seven times, but seventy-seven times."

In other words, as long as it's snowing, keep the snowplows moving.

See also: Matthew 6:14–15; 1 Corinthians 13:4–5

POINTS TO PONDER– FORGIVENESS

If you forgive men when they sin against you, your heavenly Father will also forgive you. But if you do not forgive men their sins, your Father will not forgive your sins.

MATTHEW 6:14–15

It took me a long time to learn that God is not the enemy of his enemies.

MARTIN NIEMOLLER

I think I may have to go through the agony of hearing all my sins recited in the presence of God. But I believe it will be like this—Jesus will come over and lay his hand across my shoulders and say to God, "Yes, all these things are true, but I'm here to cover up for Peter. He is sorry for all his sins, and by a transaction made between us, I am now solely responsible for them."

PETER MARSHALL

"I can forgive, but I cannot forget," is only another way of saying, "I will not forgive."

HENRY WARD BEECHER

To err is human, to forgive divine.

ALEXANDER POPE

A Christian will find it cheaper to pardon than to resent. Forgiveness saves the expense of anger, the cost of hatred, the waste of spirits.

HANNAH MORE

Everyone says forgiveness is a lovely idea, until they have something to forgive.

C. S. LEWIS

Forgiveness: the odor of flowers when they are trampled on.

ANONYMOUS

Christians aren't perfect—just forgiven.

BUMPER STICKER

If his conditions are met, God is bound by his Word to forgive any man or any woman of any sin because of Christ.

BILLY GRAHAM

Always forgive your enemies—nothing annoys them so much.

OSCAR WILDE

If we refuse mercy here, we shall have justice in eternity.

JEREMY TAYLOR

There is no use in talking as if forgiveness were easy. We all know the old joke, "You've given up smoking once; I've given it up a dozen times." In the same way I could say of a certain man, "Have

I forgiven him for what he did that day? I've forgiven him more times than I can count." For we find that the work of forgiveness has to be done over and over again.

C. S. LEWIS

To forgive somebody is to say one way or another, "You have done something unspeakable, and by all rights I should call it quits between us. Both my pride and my principles demand no less. However, although I make no guarantees that I will be able to forget what you've done and though we both carry the scars for life, I refuse to let it stand between us. I still want you for my friend." To accept forgiveness means to admit that you've done something unspeakable that needs to be forgiven, and thus both parties must swallow the same thing: their pride.

FREDERICK BUECHNER

If we are sinners forgiven, we ought to behave as forgiven, welcomed home, crowned with wonderful love in Christ, and so cheer and encourage all about us, who often go heavily because we reflect our gloom upon them instead of our grateful love, hope, confidence.

FATHER CONGREVE

Good to forgive; best to forget.

ROBERT BROWNING

See also: Isaiah 1:18; Matthew 6:12; 18:21–35; 1 John 1:9

WEEK

8

SPARK

*You will receive power when the Holy Spirit comes
on you; and you will be my witnesses in Jerusalem, and in
all Judea and Samaria, and to the ends of the earth.*

ACTS 1:8

I know that some people laugh at my idealism—
  At my effort to be a "light of the world,"
    At my eager, though often meager, attempt to
Shine a ray of brightness into an otherwise
    Dark, dank world.
There are times when I understand why people laugh and ridicule.
  I mean, how dumb can I possibly be
    To think my life really matters amidst
Four billion other people on this cinder speck of a planet
    In this distant corner of the spinning, reeling universe.
Dear God, sometimes my light seems no brighter
  Than the lambent glow of a single lightning bug
    On a very cold, black night—
      Barely a flicker, just a quick spark
    Amidst darkness deeper than shade of a shadow.
Yet a spark, just a solitary spark is all it takes
  To get a bonfire flashing and flaming, burning and blazing.
So, dear God, help me realize my life does matter,
  That being a Christian matters,
    That telling others about your greater light matters.
Teach me the secret of high-voltage living
  So that I might be your light in my world,
    Beginning at home and spreading
    To everyone within my circle of influence.
Dear God, renew in me your Holy Spirit power—
  That heavenly charge that enables mere lightning bugs
    To flame bright as lightning bolts.

See also: Matthew 5:14–16; John 14:12–14

HEALTHY HATE

Love must be sincere. Hate what is evil; cling to what is good.

ROMANS 12:9

Shortly after I became engaged to be married, panic struck. I was in love with one girl—desperately in love. Yet never before had so many other girls appealed to me. I felt like I do in a restaurant: every dish on the menu looks good, but I can have only one.

That moment was the beginning of my realization that to say yes to one girl meant I had to necessarily say no to all others. I had to wrench my affections from all who were not worthy of my complete love. And that's exactly what I did on my wedding day when I vowed to take my fiancé "to be my lawfully wedded wife and, *forsaking all others*, love her until death would us part."

The decision to "forsake all others" is central to a happy marriage. It is also central to a fulfilling relationship with God. "No one can serve two masters," Christ said. "Either he will hate the one and love the other, or he will be devoted to the one and despise the other." If our love for God is sincere, we must despise all else that hinders our relationship.

Malcolm Muggeridge describes the concept this way: "To believe greatly, it is necessary to doubt greatly." That is, if we believe in God, we must develop a radical skepticism toward all that is not godly. We must be great doubters of all that is evil if we are to be true lovers of that which is good.

To say yes to God means we must comparatively say no to *everything*, even very good things: to the United States of America, Frisbees, Julia Roberts, *Vogue*, the Ford Mustang, Sunset Beach, Brad Pitt, waffle cones, the Super Bowl, hot tubs, the Yankees,

Algebra I, bubble gum. It means we must say no to our families and, yes, especially ourselves. We can gain life only after we lose it.

"To believe greatly, it is necessary to doubt greatly." In his book *Wishful Thinking*, Frederick Buechner calls our doubts "the ants in the pants of faith." Doubts keep faith active. Doubts keep faith from settling on that which is unworthy of it. Doubts keep our love for God sincere.

See also: Mark 8:34–38; Luke 10:25–27; Titus 2:11–14

BODY TALK

> *You are the body of Christ, and each one of you is a part of it.*

> 1 CORINTHIANS 12:27

As a Christian you are a member of the worldwide family of God. Some people call this family the "universal church," consisting of believers from your classroom to the shanty huts of Nigeria. The apostle Paul calls it the "body of Christ."

Jesus is the head of this spiritual body which, like a human body, consists of hands and feet and noses and muscles and bones. Each one of us is a different part or organ, with a specific role to play.

As a writer, I may be a hand, etching out ideas on blank sheets of paper. I could start feeling inferior because I'm not as glamorous as a mouth or as critical to the body's health as a heart. On the other hand, I could feel very snooty that at least I'm not a toe, tucked inside a sweaty sock and stuffed in a shoe. But the way Paul talks, no single part is more important than any other one.

"If the whole body were an eye," Paul writes, "where would the sense of hearing be? If the whole body were an ear, where would the sense of smell be? But in fact God has arranged the parts in the body, every one of them, just as he wanted them to be."

Admittedly, Paul is no David Letterman. But I think he's trying to be funny here by saying, in effect: If you woke up one morning with a body shaped like a 150-pound ear or a monster eyeball, you'd be good for little more than the freak-show circuit. You could get a job at the circus. But the fact is, no part of the body stands alone. Every part is critical to the *whole*.

"The eye," continues Paul, "cannot say to the hand, 'I don't need you!' And the head cannot say to the feet, 'I don't need you!'"

Some of the most vital organs of the body remain out of sight—tucked deep beneath layers of skin, veins, and muscle. Yet your body would suffer greatly without them. The same is true of the body of Christ. A church with just a pastor and organist wouldn't be much of a church. The body of Christ needs *you* if it's to operate as God intended it to. If you start feeling your work is always done in the background without notice, realize that you're probably right where God wants you.

You may feel less useful than What's-his-name, but that inferiority is in your eyes only. Remember, it's *God* who "arranged the parts in the body ... just as he wanted them to be."

See also: Romans 12:3–8; 1 Corinthians 12:12–26

POVERTY

> *I was hungry and you gave me nothing to eat, I was thirsty and you gave me nothing to drink, I was a stranger and you did not invite me in, I needed clothes and you did not clothe me, I was sick and in prison and you did not look after me.*

> MATTHEW 25:42–43

For most of us, "being poor" is simply not having enough money to go out on Friday night. But there's another side, told by a young mother from Tennessee.

Here I am, dirty, smelly, with no proper underwear beneath this rotting dress. I don't know about you, but the stench of my teeth makes me half sick. They're decaying, but they'll never be fixed. That takes money.

What is poverty? Poverty is getting up every morning from a dirty and illness-stained mattress. Sheets? There are no sheets. They have long since been used for diapers, for there are no real diapers here, either. That smell? That *other* smell? You know what it is—plus sour milk and spoiled food. Sometimes it's mixed with the stench of onions cooked too often. Onions are cheap. What dishes there are, I wash in cold water. Why don't I use hot water? It takes money to heat it. Hot water is a luxury. We don't have luxuries.

Poverty is watching gnats and flies devour my baby's tears when he cries, which is much of the time. Poverty is children with runny noses, even in the summer. Paper handkerchiefs take money, and you need all your rags for other things. Antihistamines are for the rich.

Poverty is dirt. Every night I wash every stitch my school-aged child had on and just hope that the clothes will be dry enough to wear when morning comes.

Poverty is remembering—remembering quitting school in junior high because the nice children from nice homes were so cruel about your clothes and your smell.

My daughter? She'll have a life just like mine, unless she's pretty enough to become a prostitute. My boys? I can already see them behind prison bars, but it doesn't bother me as it would you. They'll be better off behind prison bars than behind the bars of my poverty. And they'll find the freedom of alcohol and drugs—the only freedom they'll know.

I leave my despair long enough to tell you this: I did not come from another place, and I did not come from another time. I'm here now, and there are others like me all around you. (Abridged from an article by C. E. Jackson, Jr. Copyright *Christian Herald.* Used by permission.)

That woman has this feeling. She thinks you're probably not interested in her life and problems. Perhaps you'd like to prove her wrong.

See also: Proverbs 31:8–9; Matthew 25:31–46; 2 Corinthians 9:6–15

DIRTY HANDS

> *Jesus said, "Simon son of John, do you truly love me?" He answered, "Yes, Lord, you know that I love you." Jesus said, "Take care of my sheep."*
>
> JOHN 21:16

Everyone has dreams. You might dream of the time you reach a certain goal or overcome a certain problem. You might dream of the time your family all become Christians, or the time Jesus returns to earth.

The lady you read about yesterday also has dreams—dreams for the time there will be money enough for the right kind of food, for medicine, for a toothbrush, for needles and thread and . . . but she knows it's just a dream, just like you know it's a dream when you see yourself as the Super Bowl MVP or the President.

Maybe you're like me. When I first read about the woman, I tried to put her out of my mind. She made me feel uncomfortable. She gave poverty a face, a personality. She gave poverty an odor. I could *smell* her life—the sour milk and spoiled food. I could smell the stink of onions cooked too often. Onions are cheap. And I could smell that *other* stench. Sure, I felt pity for her, but I knew pity wouldn't feed her children. So I simply turned the page.

But the lady never went away. Every time I opened my Bible, she was never far away. I thought of her when Jesus told Simon Peter to "Take care of my sheep." I thought of her when Jesus said, "Whatever you did for one of the least of these brothers of mine, you did for me." Yet I didn't know what to do. Should I call Goodwill and donate my bed? Should I give my lunch or movie money to those starving-children organizations? Would anything I do *really* matter?

Most of my crusades are like New Year's resolutions—somewhere along the line the promise dies. But then I got to reading in Romans and caught a glimpse of what being a Christian is all about. In Romans 8:29 Paul talks about how we're supposed to be "conformed to the likeness" of Jesus. And who was Jesus? He was proof that God didn't just feel sorry for our problems. He didn't just pat us on the head and say he cared. He put his life where his mouth was. A father may say to his sick child, "I'd do *anything* to make you better," but God actually did it.

Part of Christ's reason for coming to earth was to raise up people for whom living for others would not just be a short-term crusade, but a way of life. He sought to duplicate himself in us—to create people who would give *love* a face, a personality; people dedicated to helping dreams come true.

See also: Isaiah 53; Matthew 25:31–46; James 2:14–26

THE RISK WORTH TAKING

A crushed spirit who can bear?

PROVERBS 18:14

I grew up in San Diego where there is an abundance of beaches, and always loved the water. Sometimes I even skipped school to go surfing. And when the summer Olympics were on TV, I'd watch the swim meets for hours.

When I entered high school, I wanted to be the star swimmer on the varsity team. So I bought a pair of goggles and a bun-hugger suit, and showed up for workouts one day. But I wasn't prepared for the kind of endurance swimming the coach expected, and I nearly drowned. I eventually swam breaststroke in junior varsity meets, but even then I generally finished last. I wasn't very good at accepting failure and quit out of embarrassment.

I later tried the water polo team, but that was an equally dismal failure. I was virtually paralyzed with muscle cramps during workouts, and was cut from the tryout roster after the second week.

It wasn't until my freshman year in college that I got over the humiliation and tried out for another athletic team. At the urging of a friend, I went out for the crew team and—miraculously—discovered I was good at it. I even earned a varsity letter my first year. And that taught me something important about failure: If I hadn't tried (and risked) failure, I'd never have known my limitations or capabilities. I didn't do well at swimming or polo, but I gave athletics another chance and discovered what I could do.

That has helped me in other areas. I try not to back off from doing something because it appears too difficult or because I don't do well the first time around. When I do fail, it's an indicator I may not have talent in that specific area. But it's also an encouragement to try something else.

See also: Ecclesiastes 9:10; Isaiah 40:28–31; Hebrews 12:1–3

DIAMONDS IN THE ROUGH

We are God's workmanship, created in Christ Jesus to do good works, which God prepared in advance for us to do.

EPHESIANS 2:10

Picture God as a master jeweler and yourself as a priceless diamond in the rough. Paul probably had something like that in mind when he wrote, "We are God's workmanship." Each of us is of infinite value to the Lord. And he is at work, shaping, cutting, filing, grinding, buffing, and polishing until every facet of our lives reflects his artistry.

The shaping process is not a pleasant task, because a lot of coarse material first needs to be cut away. These rough areas may be our attitudes toward others, the way we talk, a persistent bad habit, our anger, lust, jealousy, pride, or ambition. Yet God is a gentle craftsman. He doesn't pound away with a cold chisel and sledge hammer. He works delicately and slowly, with small, precise strokes, through the convincing power of his Spirit.

So we must be patient. Gross feelings of inadequacy and inferiority will develop if we dwell on the rough sides of our character. And if we compare ourselves to other Christians, there will always be someone who seems more polished. Remember, God's work is a *process*—to be completed over a long period of time.

We are his workmanship, but as yet we're uncompleted projects. So be patient. We can't expect to be perfect and always act the right way or say the right things. We may lose our temper when provoked, talk behind someone's back, or covet another's looks, abilities, or success. God doesn't ignore these things—it's just that cutting and shaping take time. Philippians 1:6 says we can be confident "that the God who started this great work in you would keep at it and bring it to a flourishing finish on the very day Christ Jesus appears" (*The Message*).

In other words, God *will* complete the job.

See also: Philippians 2:12–13; Galatians 5:19–26

WEEK

9

THE BIG SQUEEZE

Where sin increased, grace increased all the more.

ROMANS 5:20

I feel the same familiar pressure creeping over me today, Lord. It squeezes me from the outside and eats me from the inside . . . until I feel my life would be a lot less complicated if I weren't a Christian. Nothing personal, Lord, but following you is the hardest thing I've ever attempted.

Sometimes I get tired of having to make so many choices—choices between what I want and what I think you want for me. Should I or shouldn't I wander over to that magazine rack and thumb through the latest *Playboy?* Should I or shouldn't I eat another doughnut? Should I or shouldn't I return the extra dollar the store clerk mistakenly gave me? Should I or shouldn't I join in the fun when the guys start joking about the fat girl in history class? Should I or shouldn't I have a couple of drinks at the party Friday night? Or for that matter, should I even go to the party?

All of these choices are getting to me, Lord. I mean, what do you expect? Perfection? That's kind of silly, because I don't even come close. I figure I must be just a big goof in your eyes. But then I'm confused, because the Bible is full of stories about people who even out-gross me. Your Word reads like a document of depravity, yet the losers generally come out the winners.

Rahab, the prostitute, is commended by Paul and James for her great faith. Solomon, who broke every rule in the book, later became known as the wisest man in the Bible. Moses and David were both cold-blooded killers; Noah occasionally got plastered; Peter turned his back on Christ; Sarah laughed in your face, and, well . . . talk about surprise endings!

Lord, my pressures aren't eased by knowing someone in ancient history committed murder or adultery and then went on to be listed in the Bible's Hall of Faith. But it helps me greatly to know you didn't write them off as failures just because they failed. In all their struggles and sin, they were driven back to you.

Help me do the same. Draw me back with your love when I feel like turning away and fleeing. And overwhelm me with your grace as you must have also overwhelmed Rahab, Solomon, Moses, David, Noah, Peter, Sarah, and all your other tired, life-worn, bedraggled followers.

See also: Romans 7:14–25; 2 Corinthians 4:16–18; 12:7–9

IF I HAD MY LIFE TO LIVE OVER AGAIN

Be still, and know that I am God.

PSALM 46:10

Advice from adults often begins the same way: "When I was your age ..." They somehow expect you to follow in their footsteps. But the perspective on life offered below is not so ... well, so pre-historic, and it may help you realize there are greater powers than your history teacher, who expects your oral report and 10-page paper by tomorrow. It was written late in life by an anonymous friar in a Nebraska monastery, but don't let that turn you away:

> If I had my life to live over again, I'd try to make more mistakes next time. I would relax, I would limber up, I would be sillier than I have been this trip.
>
> I know of very few things I would take seriously. I would take more trips. I would be crazier. I would climb more mountains, swim more rivers, and watch more sunsets.
>
> I would do more walking and looking. I would eat more ice cream and less beans. I would have more actual troubles, and fewer imaginary ones.

You see, I'm one of those people who lives life prophylactically and sensibly hour after hour, day after day. Oh, I've had my moments, and if I had to do it over again I'd have more of them.

In fact, I'd try to have nothing else, just moments, one after another, instead of living so many years ahead each day. I've been one of those people who never go anywhere without a thermometer, a hot-water bottle, a gargle, a raincoat, aspirin, and a parachute.

If I had to do it over again I would go places, do things, and travel lighter than I have.

If I had my life to live over I would start barefoot earlier in the spring and stay that way later in the fall. I would play hooky more. I wouldn't make such good grades, except by accident.

I would ride on more merry-go-rounds.

I would pick more daisies.

See also: Psalm 39:4–7; 100:3; Matthew 6:25–34

"NOBODIES" WANTED

The word of the Lord came to me, saying, "Before I formed you in the womb I knew you, before you were born I set you apart; I appointed you as a prophet to the nations." "Ah, Sovereign Lord," I said, "I do not know how to speak; I am only a child."

JEREMIAH 1:4–6

God had big plans for Jeremiah, as he does for each of us. That doesn't mean God has fingered you to be another "prophet to the nations," a worldwide evangelist, or a best-selling gospel singer. But he has big plans for you, nevertheless. And that may simply mean staying right where you are and being that spark of life, that ray of hope in your classroom, at home, on the racquetball court, or behind the grill flipping hamburgers for minimum wage.

With God, the size of your ministry is not important—it's your attitude toward service that matters. Are you willing to do whatever the Lord wants you to do, go wherever he wants you to go, speak to whomever he brings into your path—even if it's only the fry cook who shares your shift?

The idea of being that open to God scared Jeremiah. When God unfolded his plan for Jeremiah's life, the young man's knees rattled. He felt insecure and unqualified. He felt God had made a mistake. "I'm just a sophomore!" he might as well have said. "This is a great compliment and all, but you've got the wrong person for the job. I've never done anything like this before. Besides, I can't even talk correctly. I garble my words, mix metaphors, and st-st-stutter. Sorry, God, but it sounds like you want a superstar. I'm a nobody."

The Lord's response? "Do not say, 'I am only a child.' You must go to everyone I send you to and say whatever I command you. Do not be afraid of them for I am with you."

In a sense, none of us will ever measure up to what we *think* God needs in us. There will always be someone older, flashier, prettier, smoother—someone who could *really* win others to the Lord by the sheer magnetism of his or her personality, looks, or even testimony. But the thing is, God doesn't need superstars and leaders, as Jeremiah found out. *God* is the leader—and the only thing he needs and wants are people who, regardless of age or talent, are willing to go when he says, "Follow me!"

If you choose to follow the Lord (and make no mistake about it, it is *your* choice), you needn't worry about any limitations you think you have. His promise in Matthew 28:20 stands: "I'll be with you as you do this, day after day after day, right up to the end of the age" (*The Message*).

See also: Proverbs 3:5-6; Romans 8:31-32; Ephesians 4:10-16; 1 Peter 2:1-3

MAYBE TOMORROW

Devote yourselves to prayer, being watchful and thankful.

COLOSSIANS 4:2

I keep telling myself I need to pray more. But something always comes up. I suppose it's been weeks since I've talked with God. Maybe months. It's hard to remember.

Last night, I planned to go up to my room after dinner, dig my Bible out of my closet, and read a chapter or two. And later, spend some quality time in prayer. But the Bible was tucked under some magazines, which seemed more interesting. You know how it goes.

Then the phone rang. It was just a friend from work who wanted to switch hours. But we got to talking about that new girl on the job—the one with the California tan and cover-girl smile. When I hung up and glanced at the clock, I couldn't believe it was already time for my favorite show on TV, a two-hour special.

Before I knew it, the night was shot. I had to take a quick shower and make a sack lunch for work the next day.

It was hard to read my Bible and pray at 11:30 after all that. No energy. I tried, but kept thinking about that new girl and a thousand other things. So I ended up just mumbling a few bless 'ems before drifting off to sleep.

I know I need to pray more. I mean, to *really* pray. Other Christians I know say prayer changes things. So it must be important. But time slips away so easily. You know how it goes.

Maybe things will be different tomorrow. Yeah, maybe.

See also: Psalm 116:1-2; Matthew 7:7; 1 Thessalonians 5:17

A FAMILY MATTER

You received the Spirit of sonship. And by him we cry, "Abba, Father." The Spirit himself testifies with our spirit that we are God's children.

ROMANS 8:15–16

One day when I was traveling through England, 7,500 miles from home, I decided to call my parents. I wasn't in trouble. I didn't even need money. I simply wanted to chat.

So I tracked down the nearest phone booth, punched the international access code for direct calling and, within a few moments, heard their familiar voices. I now don't remember anything we talked about, except that at the close of conversation my father said, "Son, it's 3 a.m. here ... but we still love you. It's good just to hear your voice."

The sound of familiar voices can be very comforting. Given the emphasis the Bible places on prayer, I believe God longs just to hear our voices. And not just when we're in trouble—sometimes just to chat.

Yet people make prayer seem so formal. They prescribe everything from stance (on your knees) to timing (preferably before sunrise). Others even use a special language (Thy, Thou, Thine), while some think you can't talk to God directly—you must first go through an "operator" (such as a priest).

There's only one problem with all of this formality: Christ was often very *informal* in the way he prayed. In the Garden of Gethsemane, shortly before his crucifixion, Christ grew deeply distressed. The Bible says he fell on the ground and prayed, beginning, "Abba, Father ..." He addressed God not just as Father, but also with the Aramaic word *Abba*, meaning Daddy.

Such familiarity was not reserved solely for Christ, the Pope, and perhaps a few other spiritual Supermen and Wonderwomen.

115

According to this verse from Romans, we are God's own children. That means we have direct access to him, regardless of the time of day or night. Also, we needn't address him as "Sir!" or "Omnipotent Creator!" or "Almighty God!" *Daddy* is good enough. It's very personal—just the way you'd want to address your heavenly Father, who never tires of hearing his children's voices.

See also: Matthew 18:1–4; Mark 14:32–36; Ephesians 6:18

PROBLEMS WITH PRAYER

Pray in the Spirit on all occasions with all kinds of prayers and requests. With this in mind, be alert and always keep on praying for all the saints.

EPHESIANS 6:18

The only time I used to talk to God was when I was stretched out on my mattress, late at night. Whatever prayers I managed were punctuated by snores.

Discouraged, I shifted my prayer time to early mornings. But then, too, my mind was in a half stupor. (I tend to sputter awake in the morning, like an old car on a very cold day.)

So I got desperate. Determined to remain awake when I talked with God about things that were important to me, I started praying when I was most awake: while taking a shower. And I've done much of my praying ever since while bathing.

This developed a whole new interest in God for me. No longer did prayer seem like a chore I grudgingly put off or tried to whip through. To "pray on all occasions with all kinds of prayers ... and keep on praying" was impossible for me when I thought of God like a big shadow floating around space somewhere. It became more feasible when I realized how much prayer was like talking with a best friend—someone I wanted to be with and talk with at all times of day.

So I began to expand my prayer times. Not only did I pray in the shower, but I began to pray while driving, while jogging on the beach, while sitting in math class bored stiff. Whenever someone came to mind during the day, I immediately prayed for that person. If I felt thankful, I'd pause right then and whisper a quick "Thanks!" to God; if desperate, a quick "Help!" The spontaneity kept both my prayers fresh and me awake.

This attitude of staying in touch with God throughout the day is seen in the life of a man who called himself Brother Lawrence. In his book *The Practice of the Presence of God*, he writes that some of his closest moments with God were *not* spent on his knees. He tried to remain in constant communion with God throughout the day—and found he was sometimes most able to do that "in the noise and clatter of my kitchen, while several persons are at the same time calling for different things."

Try practicing the presence of God yourself—amidst the noise and confusion of the world you'll be facing today.

See also: Luke 18:1–8

POINTS TO PONDER—PRAYER

Pray continually.

1 THESSALONIANS 5:17

Prayer is conversation with God.

CLEMENT OF ALEXANDRIA

Tell God all that is in your heart, as one unloads one's heart to a dear friend. People who have no secrets from each other never want for subjects of conversation; they do not weigh their words, because there is nothing to be kept back. Neither do they seek for something to say; they talk out of the abundance of their hearts, just what they think. Blessed are they who attain to such familiar, unreserved intercourse with God.

FRANÇIS DE LA MOTHE FÉELON

Since the lines have been cleared between the Lord and me, the telephone has never stopped ringing.

BERNARD L. CLARK

What men usually ask for when they pray to God is that two and two may not make four.

RUSSIAN PROVERB

Seven days without prayer make one weak.

FOLK SAYING

Prayer is not an argument with God to persuade him to move things our way, but an exercise by which we are enabled by his Spirit to move ourselves his way.

LEONARD RAVENHILL

Most of us have much trouble praying when we are in little trouble, but we have little trouble praying when we are in much trouble.

RICHARD P. COOK

"Praying for particular things," said I, "always seems to me like advising God how to run the world. Wouldn't it be wiser to assume that He knows best?" "On the same principle," said he, "I suppose you never ask a man next to you to pass the salt, because God knows best whether you ought to have salt or not. And I suppose you never take an umbrella, because God knows best whether you ought to be wet or dry." "That's quite different," I protested. "I don't see why," said he. "The odd thing is that He should let us influence the course of events at all. But since He lets us do it in one way I don't see why He shouldn't let us do it in the other."

C. S. LEWIS

The fewer words the better prayer.

MARTIN LUTHER

There is nothing that makes us love a person so much as praying for him.

WILLIAM LAW

When the outlook is bad, try the uplook.

FOLK SAYING

Many a person is praying for rain with his tub the wrong side up.

SAM JONES

Much of our praying is just asking God to bless some folks that are ill, and to keep us plugging along. But prayer is not merely prattle; it is warfare.

ALAN REDPATH

The sweetest side of any fruit or vegetable is the side which grows toward the sun.

J. H. BOMBERGER

You need not cry very loud: he is nearer to us than we think.

BROTHER LAWRENCE

What a person is on his knees before God, that he is—and nothing more.

ROBERT MURRAY MCCHEYNE

See also: Proverbs 15:8; Matthew 7:7–11; Mark 11:24; Romans 8:26–27

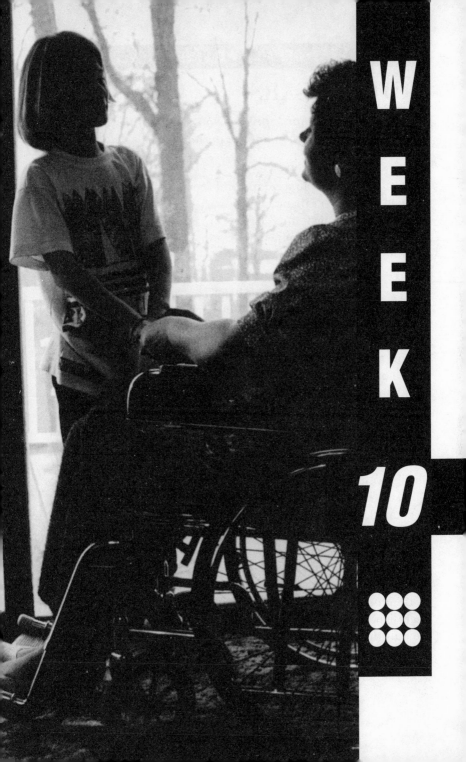

WEEK

10

FUTURE FEARS

We are hard pressed on every side, but not crushed; perplexed, but not in despair.

2 CORINTHIANS 4:8

There was a time your world seemed safe, secure. But you were much younger then. Your primary needs were met by others. Food? Clothes? The future? These were not yet concerns of yours.

But you grew, only to find your boundaries too confining. And now, you're so stifled you can't even breathe. So you thrash harder, fighting for more space—an elbow here, a knee there.

Finally, someone seems to get the message, and you slowly feel yourself being forced from your "nest." Pressures build. Your heart pounds wildly. All of the walls around you seem to collapse. There was no way to anticipate that it would be like *this*. It's all happening too fast. You try to dig in your heels to fight the pressure, but it's no use. You can't even get a fingerhold. You feel crushed by the dark tunnel you're being forced down—so scared you can't even cry.

And then, push turns to pull. Poised at the threshold of your new world, you feel cold fingers grabbing. Eyes stare. People are all smiles, but their strange faces are more like hideous masks. Panic strikes with sledgehammer force and you start to bawl. Your body shakes with each loud, racking sob.

"There, there. Everything will be all right," someone tries to comfort. But you're not so sure . . .

Congratulations! *You have just been born.*

If birth from a baby's perspective seems familiar now, it's because the feelings and sensations are not unlike those you face as you look ahead. You want to pursue your future, but you're scared of the unknown. Everything seemed so familiar, so secure a few years ago. "The Good Old Days," we call those times. Yet we know we must leave them—we must necessarily grow, develop, mature. College? Marriage? Career? These are the unfamiliar worlds toward which we grope.

We want to find God's specific will for our lives, but the process of finding it can be heartrending. There's always pressure, pain, and darkness. Yet just around the corner is a bright, new world full of new faces, challenges, and adventures.

Rest assured. Everything *will* be all right. Not because teachers, parents, pastors, or friends say so, but because *God* says so: "For I know the plans I have for you," declares the Lord, "plans to prosper you and not to harm you, plans to give you hope and a future" (Jer. 29:11).

See also: Isaiah 42:16; Hebrews 10:35–36; James 1:2–4

THE OTHER SIDE

> *Whoever wants to save his life will lose it, but whoever loses his life for me will find it.*
>
> MATTHEW 16:25

When I knew Susan, she had everything going for her: good grades, good looks, good job. Then she was in a car accident and was never the same.

I never quite understood what happened, but the drugs the doctors used to save her life apparently caused her to gain a huge amount of weight. She ballooned to two hundred and plenty pounds and lost most of her friends. Those who didn't know her just assumed she was some blimpo who gorged herself on cream pies and doughnuts. Trouble was, Susan gained weight even when she didn't eat.

"Now I know," she once told me, "how it feels to be on the other side of the fence, to feel like you're a nobody because you don't look like the girls in *Glamour*."

I later went away to college and didn't see Susan for about four years. One day after graduation I was in her area and decided to stop by. She was as big as ever, and wore a dress that looked like a Sears pup tent. But she also wore a smile that indicated she wasn't as self-conscious about her weight.

"All my life," she said, "I was programmed to think success. I had it all. And I couldn't understand why other people weren't as together as me, you know? It was like I was the yardstick, and they didn't measure up. And God may have been somewhere out there, but I didn't need him because I was doing fine on my own.

"But now I understand—that I didn't understand anything before. The needs and hurts of others? Didn't see them. Never noticed because I was all that mattered. That all changed when I became the Sumo Lady. You look like this, it's hard to have much pride.

"Now? I'm not so full of myself," she continued. "And when there's less of me, there's more room for God. The amazing thing? It's easier now to help others. To really care. To risk everything for God."

"The ironic thing?" she asked. She paused a moment and looked down. And then she came up smiling. "The irony is, I thank God for the accident. It took the car to lose myself. But that was really nothing. I lost me, but found something more important that can never be taken away."

See also: Mark 8:34–38; Luke 12:15; 1 Corinthians 10:12–13

THE SIGNAL

> *We have this hope as an anchor for the soul, firm and secure.*
>
> **HEBREWS 6:19**

I feel it coming on again: fear, crawling under my skin.
That quiet, unspoken, never-admitted feeling . . .
That haunting, ever-nagging, turn-your-back-and-run panic . . .
Fear: not of spiders or big dogs or the pull of the ocean,
But fear of my ability, people's reaction, the future, mistakes.

O Lord, help me to face my fears and turn them around.
  Be my anchor; stand by me until I—
Stop fearing I might lose in love ...
  But fear instead that I might never love at all.
Stop fearing there are others better than me ...
  But fear instead that I will never discover my true potential.
Stop fearing I might not meet others' expectations ...
  But fear instead that I might never know yours.
Stop fearing what lies ahead tomorrow, next week, next month,
next year ...
  But fear instead that I might never experience life's drama today.
Stop fearing hurt and sorrow and tears ...
  But fear instead that I will never know the pains of growth.
Stop fearing I might fail ...
  But fear instead that I might never try.
Stop fearing others will laugh at me ...
  But fear instead that I might never learn to laugh at myself.
O Lord, help me to anchor my life on your hope
  Instead of my fear.
O Lord, I know an adventurous life can never be fear-free ...
  But at least help my fears to be my soul's signal for rallying
  Instead of running.

See also: Psalm 34:4; Romans 8:15; 1 John 4:18

WORKOUT

> *Continue to work out your salvation with fear and trembling.*

PHILIPPIANS 2:12

When in training for my college rowing team, I couldn't let up. Six days a week my alarm rang at 4:30 a.m. Whether I felt like it or not, I'd drag myself out of bed and into my sweats. Breakfast was two raw eggs smooshed together in a glass of orange juice and guzzled on my way out the door.

Headlights of my old Chevy cut a swath of brightness in the black, predawn day as I headed for the boathouse for a two-hour workout before classes. After each workout, I'd be soaked with sweat, and there were many times when my hands would be raw and bloody from the constant twisting and rubbing of the oar. The salt water of Mission Bay stung my palms—until my eyes welled with tears.

Sometimes I'd sit alone in the locker room after practice and think I was crazy to stick with it. But I didn't quit because I knew it took that kind of work and determination to meet my athletic goals.

I sometimes feel a certain guilt in knowing I have not often set and pursued spiritual goals with the same relentless work and determination. There have been times I've neglected my salvation to the point of becoming spiritually flabby. Those aren't enjoyable times, because I know I've fallen short of God's standards. So I dig in and redouble my efforts to work out my salvation amidst daily battles with sin. It's not easy, but then God never promised it would be.

Being a Christian in a non-Christian world is a sweaty struggle. It's the hardest thing you'll ever do. But huge rewards await those who face the struggle, work diligently, and don't let up.

See also: 1 Corinthians 9:24–27; Hebrews 12:1–13

BUSINESS MATTERS

I have brought you glory on earth by completing the work you gave me to do.

JOHN 17:4

For years, an unfinished overpass leading nowhere arched across Highway 101 outside of San Jose, California. It spanned the freeway at a height of about 70 feet, but stopped abruptly with steel rods poking like spaghetti from either end. All construction equipment had been removed from the site, and the towering mass of concrete and twisted steel served as a sort of monument to "unfinished business."

Whenever I passed beneath that "overpass to nowhere," I thought of the unfinished business lingering in my life: the books half read, thank-you letters never mailed, and paintbrushes never cleaned. Perseverance in such day-to-day projects is important, but there are two areas in which our commitment to completion is even more crucial: *People Projects* and *God Projects*.

People Projects. Is there a friend you have unfinished business with—maybe someone you wronged and need to ask forgiveness from? Perhaps there's a classmate you said you'd pray for, but never did. Is there someone you need to befriend—perhaps that quiet girl who always sits alone at lunch? When did you last tell anyone *sincerely*, "I love you"?

God Projects. Unfinished business here includes secret sins you may still be holding onto—parts of your life you'd like others and especially God not to know about. Perhaps you made a vow to God that you never kept. Have you abandoned any spiritual goals? Are there friends or family members you've neglected to tell about Jesus Christ and salvation?

In the 33 years Christ lived on earth, he fulfilled God's every purpose for his life. He loved the unlovable, healed the sick, rejected temptation . . . and pointed people to God. Toward the end of his life he could rightfully say, "I have brought you glory on earth by completing the work you gave me to do."

But there was one last matter. It was necessary that he die on the cross for our sin. And as he hung there, he cried his final words, "It is finished!"

He had no unfinished business. Do you?

See also: Luke 14:28–33; Hebrews 12:1–3

SECOND NATURE

Those who hope in the Lord will renew their strength. They will soar on wings like eagles; they will run and not grow weary, they will walk and not be faint.

ISAIAH 40:31

A simple task like walking is not something you probably give much thought to—unless, of course, you've injured yourself badly enough to require therapy. And then you feel like a squat-legged infant again: wiggly and rubber-kneed as you first learn to balance. Very slowly and very painfully you progress to the step-rock-step-rock pattern that is, for most people, second nature—as simple as breathing.

The same is true of any learned task. As I work now at my computer to compose this paragraph, I do not fret about where to place my fingers, or hunt and peck to find certain letters. Years ago, that keyboard looked impossibly complex. But with a certain amount of training and coaching, typing became second nature.

No one needs to tell you there are times when being a Christian in a non-Christian world feels next to impossible. You face temptations that blitz your mind daily: things like lust and sex, a chance for revenge, use of a credit card, a second helping of cream pie. You feel discouraged, beat, and wonder if there's any hope for you. *Will you ever be spiritual?* You wonder about God. Will he finally just give up on you and stomp off, leaving you to manage on your own?

It's appropriate that Christ referred to the act of becoming a Christian as being "born again." In God's eyes you are a newborn infant—and he wants to train you . . . his way. That training process is difficult. At times, very difficult. But God has not left you to blunder your way in darkness like some sadistic father who turns the

128

light out on his wobble-kneed infant and then laughs when the kid smashes into a table.

Rather, "God works in you to will and act according to his good purpose." That's to say he helps you in your Christian walk, and he's there to pick you up again if you fall. It's when you take his outstretched hand and follow him that walking feels like second nature. And it's then that you feel most able to not just *walk*, but to "*s*oar on wings like eagles" and *run* and not grow weary."

See also: Philippians 2:12–13; 1 John 1:5–7

BORN AGAIN

I tell you the truth, unless a man is born again, he cannot see the kingdom of God.

JOHN 3:3

Some would describe Christians as people who *believe* certain things. For example, that Jesus was born in a Middle Eastern cow stable. That he turned water into wine. That church is a good place to hang out on Sundays.

Others would describe Christians as those who *do* or *don't do* certain things. They talk to God. They don't tell dirty jokes. They read the Bible. They don't smoke in school restrooms.

Still others would describe Christians as basically *good* people. They send birthday cards to their grandma. They actually sing the "Star-Spangled Banner" at ball games. They turn in homework on time. They smile a lot.

But Jesus had something else in mind. He described Christians as those who have been "born again." When he first used the term, he was speaking with Nicodemus, a head Jew who was big in religious politics. At first, Nicodemus didn't understand what Jesus was talking about. It triggered a ridiculous image in his mind of a grown person curling into a fetal ball and reentering his mother's womb to be reborn. But Christ was not trying to be funny when he used the analogy. He wanted to convey some key spiritual concepts.

For one thing, your spiritual birth (like your physical birth) marked a new beginning for you in a new world. As W. A. Criswell notes, "Christianity is the land of beginning again." You were given a new father, a new home, a new family. That is, a whole new identity. As the early Christians said of each other, you've become a "new creation."

Sure, you still look the same in a mirror. Your outer characteristics don't change. But your inner characteristics do. As you get to know God better, some of his personality and traits rub off on you. It's not a conscious thing. One day you simply notice that some things you once enjoyed now seem empty and pointless. Things such as attending wild parties, getting plastered, or making crude jokes about others no longer have the same attraction they once might have. You also notice things such as a new-found sense of hope and peace about the future. Or perhaps a changing attitude toward others—your parents, for example.

At the heart of the "born again" analogy is the idea that there's nothing you could ever have done to "earn" or "deserve" God. Being a Christian is not something you do or think. Being a Christian is not living idealistically and doing good deeds. It's a relationship. Like physical birth, spiritual birth stems from an act of love that precedes delivery. It's through Jesus, and Jesus alone, that we've become sons and daughters of God.

Welcome to the family!

See also: 2 Corinthians 5:17; Ephesians 2:1–10; 4:17; 5:21

WEEK 11

HOT UNDER THE COLLAR

In your anger do not sin: Do not let the sun go down while you are still angry, and do not give the devil a foothold.

EPHESIANS 4:26–27

You're already late to class when that big-eared jock on the wrestling team blindsides you and sends your books flying.

"Hey, be careful or you'll drop your books," he laughs and keeps walking.

You scramble to pick up your ego and scattered belongings from the hall floor, feeling that familiar fire of anger creep up your neck. Your nerves go taut and your heart starts twanging away. You feel like jumping the bum and landing a haymaker to his head.

Such feelings are automatic and normal—you shouldn't feel uncomfortable that they exist. God didn't create you like a power-cooled, controlled-temperature Whirlpool fridge. But you do have a choice in how you *respond* to anger and other strong emotions. Paul suggests it's possible to respond in a way that doesn't go against God.

Your first impulse is to get revenge, if only to yell, "You stupid lughead, can't you see where you're going!" You want to stick up for your rights—to save face. But considering the guy's size, you realize you'll probably *lose* face if a fight were to break out.

Regardless of size, James suggests we ought to be "slow to speak and slow to become angry." Mark Twain had a comment on this matter: "When angry, count four; when very angry, swear." Maybe you should instead count to 10 or take a couple of deep breaths. The more time you have to think about your response, the less hurtful it will be.

"A gentle answer turns away wrath," wrote Solomon in Proverbs. In other words, be creative in an explosive situation. Adding fuel to a fire just makes a bigger fire. Dealing with people is much the same. You can often diffuse a potentially explosive situation with a touch of humor. For instance, you might try something like: "Hey, Mack, roller derby practice doesn't start for another week!"

However you respond, Paul suggests you deal with anger within the day. Stewing overnight may be great for a slab of barbecue meat. But with people it's the recipe for an ulcer.

See also: Proverbs 15:1; James 1:19–20

PAPIER-MÂCHÉ FACADE

Through Christ our comfort overflows.

2 CORINTHIANS 1:5

When Christa's parents divorced, she wasn't surprised. There had been plenty of clues—the fights, the drinking, the accusations about unfaithfulness. But she was surprised by the volcanic feelings that erupted within her, especially since she considered herself a "strong" Christian.

Christa knew it was normal for Christians to feel crummy at times—as if their world were caving in. But she was afraid to talk to anyone about the depths of her despair, because she didn't know what they would think. Her friends had always considered her level-headed and emotionally calm. What would they say if they knew she was just hiding her feelings behind a papier-mâché smile that was beginning to crack?

Then one night as she lay crying in bed, she began to talk to God about the problems she faced. If anyone understood, she figured he would. She told God of her anger, bitterness, and confusion. She told him she felt totally crushed by her parents' situation and didn't think she loved her father. She told God there was something inside her that craved a daddy's shoulder to cry on, for a daddy's arms to hold her and give her a sense of confidence. Without that, she told God, she didn't feel like a whole person.

As weeks passed, God became that father she could turn to. That's not to say the going was easy. It was especially hard to cope during the lonely, stare-at-the-ceiling hours before she could fall asleep at night. She was still hurt. But she felt God wanted to help. By opening her heart to him, she gained the security and confidence to face her problems and the support to work them out.

See also: Psalm 5; 23; Matthew 11:28–30; John 14:27

A MATTER OF THANKS

Give thanks in all circumstances, for this is God's will for you in Christ Jesus.

1 THESSALONIANS 5:18

The day after Christmas was always the same around my house. My mom would start hassling me to write thank-you letters for gifts I'd received. Grandparents, aunts and uncles, cousins I hardly knew—everyone was due a note of thanks. Eventually—at least by March—I'd get the last of the cards mailed.

It's not just people we forget to thank. We often neglect God, too. Take some time to write a letter of thanks to God for the greatest gifts of all: his son, his forgiveness, his love. Perhaps there are other things you'd also like to thank him for.

Dear God,

I'd just like to say thanks for _____

_____

_____

I'd also like to thank you for _____

_____

_____

The gifts you've given me have really made a difference in my life. For example, _____

_____

_____

In closing, I'd just like to say: _____

_____

Love always,

_____

See also: John 3:16; Luke 17:11–19: Romans 6:23; 8:28

THE DECIDING VOTE

> *The high priest asked him, "Are you the Christ, the Son of the Blessed One?" "I am," said Jesus. "And you will see the Son of Man sitting at the right hand of the Mighty One and coming on the clouds of heaven."*
>
> MARK 14:61–62

Imagine you're at Rockefeller Plaza in the concrete jungle of New York City, sitting in a black vinyl chair behind a wall of glass marked PERSONNEL. You fidget nervously with the small tear in the armrest as the somber-faced interviewer reviews your job application and then says, "For starters, tell me something about yourself."

To his infinite surprise you blurt, "Well, I'm Rocky's son." He stares at you, and then breaks into a deep, low chuckle. At which you reply, "And someday I'll be his chief aide—his right-hand man." Your interviewer now has a choice to make. Are you a Rockefeller or a fake? Chances are he'd decide the latter and notify security.

A similar situation existed when Christ stood before an elite gathering of chief priests and elders—the religious honchos of his day. In effect, they asked him to recite his résumé. His reply? He claimed to be the Son of God. And if that wasn't crazy enough, he said he would one day sit at God's right hand.

The inquisitors, at that point, had a decision to make: to either bow or give him a knuckle sandwich. Mark, one of Christ's twelve disciples, described what followed: "They all condemned him as worthy of death. Then some began to spit at him; they blindfolded him, struck him with their fists, and said, 'Prophesy!' And the guards took him and beat him." The cross was not far behind.

Jesus' claims of kinship with God led some to reject and eventually kill him. Those same words—and the life that backed them up—motivated others to alter their lives radically, to serve him ... and even to die for him.

Some 2,000 years later that choice still stands. Is he King of kings or Kook of kooks? His bizarre claims demand a verdict. And you've got the deciding vote.

See also: Matthew 27:41–43; John 10:24–38

THE MAYOR IS MOVING!

For you know the grace of our Lord Jesus Christ, that though he was rich, yet for your sakes be became poor, so that you through his poverty might become rich.

2 CORINTHIANS 8:9

Cabrini Green—if you'd ever want a taste of hell, this sprawling public-housing project in Chicago would be a good place to start. Sharp rat-a-tat bursts of gunfire echo regularly through its 81 high-rises and row houses. Mysterious screams split the night, but no one dares to investigate. Gangs exercise total control of the estimated 14,000 people living there—raping, extorting, and murdering those who get in their way.

During the winter when I lived in a nearby suburb, Chicago's mayor made a much-publicized tour of Cabrini Green and told its terrorized residents, "You are going to live in security and safety." It seemed like a typical comment from a typical politician. Didn't the nut realize that even Chicago's police were powerless amidst the guns, gangs, and terror?

The following week, the mayor took things a step further and announced plans to temporarily move to Cabrini Green to see firsthand the problems of that crime-ridden neighborhood. City politicians said they'd never heard anything like it before. "It is a pretty dramatic thing to do," said one. MAYOR MOVING TO CABRINI! headlines screamed.

As I followed the story over the succeeding months, I couldn't help but think how Christ did much the same thing when he vacated heaven to live on earth. I imagine some of the angels thought it too radical and dangerous. They would have been right on both accounts.

But Christ knew he had to visit our planet to make it possible for us to experience life in all its glory—a taste of heaven in the midst of hell.

See also: John 3:16; 14:27; Philippians 2:3–11

WITH APOLOGIES TO LUKE

> *The angel said to them, "Do not be afraid. I bring you good news of great joy that will be for all the people."*
>
> LUKE 2:10

And it came to pass in those days, that there went out a decree from managers of all department stores, large and small, that first payments on all Christmas purchases be delayed until February 1.

And the news met people with gladness, and they all went to their nearest Nordstroms, Saks, and, yea, even to Wal-Mart and Kmart, to freely buy. And they brought forth their packages, wrapped in colored tissues and bright ribbon, and laid them beneath their artificial trees; because that was fitting and proper during the yuletide.

And there were in the same season children abiding beside their bedroom windows, keeping watch over the skies by night. And lo, the glory of Saint Nick shone round about them, and they were sore afraid.

And the rotund little man said unto them, "Fear not. For behold, I bring you good news of great joy that will be for all children of affluent homes. For unto you will be given at dawn, computerized toys and dolls and train sets."

And it came to pass, the morning after the appearance, the children screamed with delight when they saw the gifts, and made known to their elders the message foretold the previous night.

Indeed, the elders knew their children had merely dreamed dreams; at their young ages they were sheltered from the true reality of credit cards, finance charges, and overdrawn accounts. And the children's parents kept all these things, and pondered them heavily within their hearts.

See also: Matthew 6:19–24; 1 Timothy 6:6–10

POINTS TO PONDER—THE INCARNATION

Today in the town of David a Savior has been born to you; he is Christ the Lord.

LUKE 2:11

Since Christ's birth some 2,000 years ago, much has been written about this God/man and those years when he walked in our shoes. Planet Earth never had such a visitor, and writers have never gotten over it:

You can never truly enjoy Christmas until you can look up into the father's face and tell him you have received his Christmas gift.

JOHN R. RICE

The hinge of history is on the door of a Bethlehem stable.

RALPH W. SOCKMAN

Santa Claus never died for anybody.

CRAIG WILSON

A man who was merely a man and said the sort of things Jesus said wouldn't be a great moral teacher. He'd either be a lunatic—on a level with a man who says he's a poached egg—or else he'd be the devil of hell. You must make your choice. Either this man was, and is, the son of God, or else a madman or something worse.

C. S. LEWIS

Christ is greater than our faith in him.

JAMES HASTINGS

Christmas is not just the birth of a baby; it is the heavenly father saying good-bye to his son.

ANONYMOUS

I sometimes think we expect too much of Christmas Day. We try to crowd into it the long arrears of kindliness and humanity of the whole year. As for me, I like to take my Christmas a little at a time, all through the year.

DAVID GRAYSON

A man may go to heaven without health, without riches, without honors, without learning, without friends; but he can never go there without Christ.

JOHN DYER

Christ is the great central fact in the world's history. To him everything looks forward or backward. All the lines of history converge upon him. All the great purposes of God culminate in him. The greatest and most momentous fact which the history of the world records is the fact of his birth.

CHARLES H. SPURGEON

Christmas is a son away from home.

NORMA ALLOWAY

I wish we could put some of the Christmas spirit in jars and open a jar of it every month.

GERALD STANLEY LEE

It is Christmas in the heart that puts Christmas in the air.

W. T. ELLIS

God and I have this in common—we both love his son, Jesus Christ.

LANCE ZAVITZ

You needn't worry about not feeling brave. Our Lord didn't—see the scene in Gethsemane. How thankful I am that when God became man he did not choose to become a man of iron nerves; that would not have helped weaklings like you and me nearly so much.

C. S. LEWIS

Questions about Christ's identity haven't changed much in 2,000 years. Either he was a full-tilt crazy with the asylum key, or he carried the key to unlock the entire universe. The choice is yours: Kook of kooks or King of kings.

S. RICKLY CHRISTIAN

See also: Luke 1:26–38; 2:1–20

WEEK

12

MARKS OF A CHRISTIAN

The fruit of the Spirit is love, joy, peace, patience,
kindness, goodness, faithfulness, gentleness and self-con-
trol. Against such things there is no law.

GALATIANS 5:22–23

Outwardly, Christians look like any other people you'd pass in the locker hall or mall. They don't wear uniforms and salute, like Scouts and soldiers. They don't all have the same weird kind of hairstyle, like Hare Krishna cultists. They don't wear special jackets or rings or have special handshakes, like members of some club or gang. They don't go to the same church, drive the same car, or listen to the same music.

So you might wonder: What's the big difference between a Christian and a non-Christian?

The Bible is clear that there should be very distinguishing characteristics. "If anyone is in Christ," the apostle Paul wrote, "he is a new creation; the old has gone, the new has come." In other words, when people become Christians, their insides are transformed. They aren't quite the same anymore. New life has begun!

This transformation occurs from the inside out. Christianity is not a fish insignia on your car or a gushy "Praise the Lord!" or hands held high in church. It's a seed of faith planted in the heart. And as that seed is nurtured, it begins to grow and sprout what Paul calls "fruit of the Spirit."

These nine characteristics—love, joy, peace, patience, kindness, goodness, faithfulness, gentleness, and self-control—are the marks of a true Christian. They are an indication that the seed of faith has sprouted and new life has begun. (In the following two-and-a-half weeks, we'll take a closer look at each of these characteristics. And you'll have an opportunity to take a personal inventory to determine how much "fruit of the Spirit" is growing in your life.)

No, you can't spot Christians in a mirror or across a crowded cafeteria. But they *are* somehow different. The next pages will describe a few of the ways *you* should be different.

See also: Matthew 7:15–23

MARKS OF A CHRISTIAN–LOVE

The fruit of the Spirit is love.

GALATIANS 5:22

Of the nine "fruits of the Spirit" mentioned by Paul in the passage you read yesterday, love tops the list. It is not just another mark of a Christian, but the *birthmark* of a Christian—sort of like God's thumbprint in your life.

When asked what the greatest commandment was, Christ replied, "Love the Lord your God with all your heart and with all your soul and with all your mind." The second, he said, was like it: "Love your neighbor as yourself." In other words, your life as a Christian should be marked first by your love for God, and then by your love for others and yourself.

Love for God. If you think of God as a great shadow or force that flits about with the satellites, it will be difficult loving him. The Bible is clear that God is not some nebulous, celestial power, but a person as real as your best friend. That's why Christianity is not a religion, but a *relationship*. Your love for God can be measured by the amount of time you want to spend with him and by how much you allow him to influence your life. Is he a secret friend you're ashamed of, or is he someone you eagerly introduce others to? Have you told God you love him during the past week? He wants to know!

Love for others. Love loves the unlovely, the unloving, the unlovable. It doesn't care if it's loved in return. Said Christ, "Love your enemies and pray for those who persecute you.... If you love

143

those who love you, what reward will you get?" Christian love turns a blind eye toward others' faults and keeps no record of wrong. It's patient, kind, and never fails.

Love for yourself. Many people have trouble with this. They wear many masks and try to appear smooth and controlled. But inside they're full of low self-esteem, perhaps because of their upbringing or because their looks or abilities don't measure up to those around them. Self-love is the recognition that you're a unique creation of God. He made *you* for a reason—with every scar and idiosyncrasy. You can love and accept yourself, because God first loved you!

"All mankind loves a lover," wrote Ralph Waldo Emerson. And as a Spirit-filled Christian, you should be the world's greatest!

See also: Ephesians 3:14–20

MARKS OF A CHRISTIAN—LOVE

The fruit of the Spirit is love.

GALATIANS 5:22

Shortly before Christ went to the cross, he gave his disciples some final instructions on living as Christians after he was gone.

"I will be with you only a little longer," he began, and then launched into his favorite topic. "A new commandment I give you: Love one another. As I have loved you, so you must love one another." Jesus probably paused at this point before adding the clincher: "All men will know that you are my disciples *if you love one another.*" In this verse, Jesus gives everyone who knows you the right to judge the validity of your Christianity . . . based on your love for others.

With this in mind, consider that you've just been arrested for being a Christian. Could the prosecutors build a case (based solely on your observable love toward others) to find you guilty?

Take a few minutes to jot down some of the evidence they would present against you in court:

_____

_____

_____

_____

_____

What does the above evidence suggest about your Christianity? Do you have enough "fruit of love" in your life to be convicted?

See also: John 13:33–35; 1 Thessalonians 3:12

MARKS OF A CHRISTIAN–JOY

The fruit of the Spirit is . . . joy.

GALATIANS 5:22

If one of the distinguishing marks of a Christian is supposed to be joy, you wonder what went wrong. Why is it that many people view believers as a gloomy bunch of pious poops with personalities like soggy Cream of Wheat? They equate Christianity with suit-and-tie churchiness, nose-in-the-air stuffiness. What was meant to be a relationship that's full of joy has, in many cases, deteriorated to a form of religion full of stiff formality.

Somber Christians daily display the "costs" of following Christ: They've given up drinking, smoking, swearing, fornicating, and fighting. But they've also given up smiling and laughing and having genuine good ol' times every day of the week.

This is not a recent problem. Jesus frequently had confrontations with the stuffy, religious people of his day—people who thought they knew all about God, but didn't know how to live, laugh, or love. On days of fasting, they displayed drawn, hollow-eyed looks so others would recognize their sacrifice. They gushed flowery prayers and stood sad-eyed on street corners to advertise their supposed holiness. Their misery was infectious, because many people have been following their example ever since.

But Christianity isn't for deadheads. At least if you take Christ as the model. He was not so much a "man of sorrows" as a man of joy. We know he didn't stifle his tears—but he also didn't cover up his laughter and joy. He liked parties and fun and swarms of kids—because it was for things like this that the rigid Pharisees most criticized him. The stories he told were often of joyous feasts and celebrations. He likened the kingdom of God not to a convention of bleary-eyed librarians, but to a rollicking banquet and a wedding feast—tremendous times of joy. And some of his most widely reported miracles (turning water into wine and multiplying the fish and loaves) were done for the pleasure of those around him.

Joy was indeed "serious business" with Christ. And if you're filled with his Spirit, you also ought to be filled with his joy!

See also: Psalm 100; Romans 15:13

MARKS OF A CHRISTIAN—JOY

The joy of the Lord is your strength.

NEHEMIAH 8:10

When you think of the word "joy," chances are you equate it with some sort of emotional high or outward jollity. You might think of how you feel when a teacher tells you, "The test is canceled," or the rush you experience when kissed by someone other than your grandma. It might be when your braces come off, you win a big race, or get accepted to college. You might think of smiles and laughter and good times.

But joy is much more than all of these things. It's not a fleeting feeling that's here today, gone tomorrow. You can be down in the dumps and still have joy. Consider the story of Job. His crops, flocks, herds, and home were destroyed, his servants and family were killed, and *he* broke out with excruciating boils "from the soles of his feet to the top of his head." A boil is like a grape-sized pimple. If you've ever had one, you can imagine the torture Job felt with thousands—even in his armpits and between his toes. Yet he still spoke of his "joy in unrelenting pain" (Job 6:10).

As for Jesus, he spoke about joy over a very sad dinner with a group of his best friends. The occasion: his "going away" supper—the last meal he had before the Roman goon squad nailed him to a cross. Jesus was more or less saying his good-byes, and everyone in the room, including him, was probably bawling and sobbing like a baby. But he didn't mention the tears. He talked about joy (John 15:11).

Joy doesn't depend on good times. If it did, many people would be left out. It doesn't depend on good luck or good news—both of which are fleeting and often outweighed by bad luck or bad news. It doesn't depend on smiles, which are skin deep. Joy is soul deep, and should be evidenced in your life when you can find nothing to smile about.

How has your understanding of joy changed? Jot down a few of your new concepts in the space below:

_____

_____

_____

_____

_____

_____

See also: 2 Corinthians 7:4; Hebrews 12:2–3; James 1:2–4

MARKS OF A CHRISTIAN—PEACE

The fruit of the Spirit is ... peace.

GALATIANS 5:22

I once read about two artists who were commissioned to paint a picture signifying their individual concepts of perfect peace.

The first artist pulled on his boots and hiked into the Rockies outside Boulder, Colorado. Several miles beyond the nearest ski lift, he erected his easel beside a secluded lake known only to locals. Poised in this Hallmark-perfect setting, he filled his canvas with the lace-like haze of early morning as it dissolved before the first golden rays of daylight. The brilliant greens of the towering pines were so vivid in the painting that the artist's oils seemed to smell of the forest. A hawk floated lazily across the sky, its image reflected in the mirror of the lake's still surface. It was the kind of picture you'd expect to see on a greeting card or on the cover of your grandpa's *Reader's Digest.*

The second artist applied for press credentials, hopped a red-eye flight for war-torn Lebanon, and set his easel near the gutted building which then served as headquarters of the terrorist Palestine Liberation Organization. Shielded by a heap of bricks and twisted girders, the artist filled his canvas with a fiery maelstrom as violent as that which fell from the bombers overhead. Rockets cut a swath of destruction across the painting—so lifelike that explosions and screams seemed to roar with each stroke of his brush. But there, just outside the ruins in the crook of a bent little tree, was a bird resting atop a nest of eggs. Seemingly insulated from the chaos all about, it sat with its tiny head tucked serenely beneath its wing.

The second artist was the one who captured the essence of genuine peace—the kind of peace Christ offers those who heed his call, "Come to me, all you who are weary and burdened, and I will give you

148

rest." His rest doesn't come in an isolated setting where you are immune from people and problems. It comes when you need it most. Being a Christian doesn't guarantee you freedom from hardships and confusion. For many, it seems to *ensure* them. But in the middle of difficulties you face at home, work, or school, God will help develop the "fruit of peace" in your life. That is, peace amidst your biggest wars.

See also: Psalm 4:8; Matthew 11:28–30

MARKS OF A CHRISTIAN–PEACE

> *Peace I leave with you; my peace I give you. I do not give to you as the world gives. Do not let your hearts be troubled and do not be afraid.*
>
> JOHN 14:27

Peace for some people means a six-pack of beer or a couple of joints. Others try to overcome hassles by going on an eating binge and downing a carton of Ding Dongs. Some play mental gymnastics with their problems and wind up with ulcers from worrying. Others try to vent their frustrations by screaming a lot or going on a spending spree. There are as many ways to find peace as there are people seeking it.

But Christ said that only one way works. His way. The peace he gives is different from what the world gives. Take some time today to write down what some of those differences are. Use the space below. The verses on the next page can help give you some ideas.

The World Says PEACE Is:	The Bible Says PEACE Is:
A wild party on Friday night	_____
Enough drugs	_____
The latest issue of *Penthouse*	_____
_____	_____
_____	_____

Honestly evaluate your own life. Which side of the line most accurately describes your response to stress and hassles? Begin working with God to make his "Peace Plan" more evident within you.

See also: Psalm 23; Matthew 6:25–34; Philippians 4:6–7

WEEK

13

MARKS OF A CHRISTIAN— PATIENCE

The fruit of the Spirit is ... patience.

GALATIANS 5:22

Patience: It's an odd word in this "aspirin age" where relief from pain and problems is just two pills and a swallow of water away. In a society that pioneered "presto living" through such everyday commodities as microwaves, frozen gourmet dinners, and minute rice, patience seems like some concept from a time warp—as out-dated as typewriters and phonograph records.

Yet the Bible's standards haven't changed. Patience is the trademark stamp of God's Holy Spirit in your life. As with love, joy, peace, and the other fruit of the Spirit, God wants to grow more patience in your life: patience to persist when you fail the first time; patience to endure hardship and personal struggles without griping, knowing you'll somehow be stronger in the end; patience to listen when your parents ramble about "back when I was your age ..."

Patience is not honking when stuck on the freeway behind the little old lady from Pasadena; it's not kicking a hole in the door when locked out by your kid sister. Patience is waiting for God's absolute best in your life, whether a marriage partner or a job. This kind of patience will not sprout overnight. The making of a Christian who is Christlike is a timely process that God does not rush.

The book of James talks a lot about patience. James launches the first chapter with the words: "Consider it a sheer gift, friends, when tests and challenges come at you from all sides. You know that under pressure, your faith-life is forced into the open and shows its true colors" (*The Message*). It's important that we let pressure do its work, he adds, "so you become mature and well-developed, not deficient in any way." In other words, the hardships you'd prefer to sidestep are the very things you should patiently and joyfully endure.

Grit your teeth, but don't forget to smile! Don't let your daily problems at home, work, or school drive you to panic—let them drive you joyfully to patience ... and to a closer relationship with Christ. As a Christian, you are to be what Amy Carmichael calls "the Lord's diehards, to whom can be committed any kind of trial of endurance, and who can be counted upon to stand firm whatever happens."

James closes his book on the same topic: "You see farmers do this all the time, waiting for their valuable crops to mature, patiently letting the rain do its slow but sure work. Be patient like that. Stay steady and strong." Don't give up or give in—the fruit of patience is well worth the wait.

See also: Romans 12:12; Hebrews 12:1–12

MARKS OF A CHRISTIAN— PATIENCE

Be patient, bearing with one another in love.

EPHESIANS 4:2

Perhaps you've seen those lapel buttons that read: "PBPGIN-FWMY." *Please be patient—God is not finished with me yet.* You are God's special project—he is at work in your life, but he's not done.

Just as God hasn't given up on you, so you shouldn't give up on others who also are God's workmanship. Each person (Christian or not) is of infinite value to the Lord—created in God's image—and in each, his "construction project" is at a different stage of completion. Knowing how patient God has been with you should help you demonstrate patience toward others and enable you to "bear with one another in love," as Paul writes.

Take a few minutes to think about ways in which God has shown patience toward you. Your life has undoubtedly changed since you became a Christian, but what areas still need work? List some of these "hot spots" below:

_____

_____

God works patiently. He doesn't spot something negative in your life and then twist your arm or beat you with a stick until you make it right. He loves you until you, of your own free will, decide you want what he wants. God's patience toward you is not unique—it's how he responds to everyone because patience is part of his character. And he wants it to be part of yours, too.

Think of people who most try your patience: the motor-mouth in English, your slob brother, your nice but overbearing Aunt Anita. With their names in mind, jot down a few ideas about how you might be more patient with them:

_____

_____

In the days to come, ask God to help you practice patience—to be the "Lord's diehard" toward these people.

See also: Ephesians 2:10; Philippians 1:4–6; 2 Peter 3:9, 15

MARKS OF A CHRISTIAN—KINDNESS

The fruit of the Spirit is ... kindness.

GALATIANS 5:22

Kindness doesn't take a lot of time or ingenuity. It is such a little, seemingly inconsequential, thing. Yet this mark of a Christian in your life will help make life for others seem consequential. That's because little things matter to most people—things like a warm smile, encouraging word, or squeeze of the hand. Without such gestures, their lives become a blur of uninterrupted days; with them, moments punctuated by exclamation points.

Kindness is an offer to help clean up after the dog, a "thank-you" note, a whispered "I love you." Kindness is listening to someone who hasn't brushed his teeth in days, a handful of flowers given "just because," a careful compliment, a word of praise. Kindness is taking your kid sister and her giggly-faced friends to the bowling alley and staying to laugh with them later over Cokes, consoling the new kid who just moved from Indiana, talking computers with the geek who walks like an old man with tight shoes.

Kindness is refraining from saying something you have every right to say, dropping "you always" and "you never" from your vocabulary, letting your dad be right. Kindness is letting someone else go first, ignoring a fault, holding no grudge. Kindness is allowing Christ to work through you to touch lives and show compassion in very ordinary ways.

In the back of my Bible is a yellowed sheet of paper containing a somewhat musty poem by an unknown author. Though the style is dated, the words never will be:

Is anybody happier because you passed his way?
Does anyone remember that you spoke to him today?
This day is almost over, and its toiling time is through.
Is there anyone to utter now a friendly word for you?
Can you say tonight in passing with the days that slipped so fast,
That you helped a single person, of the many that you passed?
Is a single heart rejoicing over what you did or said?
Does one whose hopes were fading now with courage look ahead?
Did you waste the day, or lose it? Was it well or poorly spent?
Did you leave a trail of kindness or a scar of discontent?

See also: Hebrews 13:2

155

MARKS OF A CHRISTIAN– KINDNESS

If anyone gives even a cup of cold water to one of these little ones because he is my disciple, I tell you the truth, he will certainly not lose his reward.

MATTHEW 10:42

Small acts of kindness seem so inconsequential. In the verse above, a cup of cold water is such a little thing. Yet Christ indicates that it pays big dividends. Later on (Matt. 25:34–46), Christ explains that kindness to others is an act of love toward God:

"The King will say ..., 'I was hungry and you gave me something to eat, I was thirsty and you gave me something to drink, I was a stranger and you invited me in, I needed clothes and you clothed me, I was sick and you looked after me, I was in prison and you came to visit me.'

"Then the righteous will answer him, 'Lord, when did we see you hungry and feed you, or thirsty and give you something to drink? When did we see you a stranger and invite you in, or needing clothes and clothe you? When did we see you sick or in prison and go to visit you?'

"The King will reply, 'I tell you the truth, whatever you did for one of the least of these brothers of mine, you did for me.'"

Such simple things are the very things that matter to God ... and make a Christian stand apart from the crowd. Feeding the hungry, giving your jacket to someone shivering, sharing your room with someone homeless, visiting the sick or imprisoned—such acts reap great rewards. Your trail of kindness leads straight to God.

In the coming week, experiment with kindness to see what a difference it really makes to other people, and how good it feels to you. Your project? Demonstrate small acts of kindness *anonymously* to: (1) each member of your family, (2) a neighbor, (3) someone you don't like, and (4) a stranger.

If they find out that it was you, it doesn't count—you'll have to be kind to them all over again!

See also: Proverbs 25:21–22

MARKS OF A CHRISTIAN— GOODNESS

The fruit of the Spirit is . . . goodness.

GALATIANS 5:22

The news report went something like this: "John Wayne Gacy was arrested this morning on charges stemming from the recent murders of several young Cook County boys." Police eventually pinned Gacy with the brutal slayings of nine youths, but they unearthed 27 bodies from shallow graves in the crawl space beneath his home and linked him with the murders of five others. Long paragraphs related the details of the grisly crimes, followed by quotes from surprised neighbors, such as: "He *seemed* like such a good man. He even helped out with the neighborhood carnival." Perhaps John Gacy had also once helped a neighbor fix her car, given a child a cookie, or taken a group of Scouts on an outing. Based on a few isolated acts of goodness, neighbors assumed the best and were horrified when his inner character bubbled to the surface.

Trouble is, there's a big difference between doing some particular good thing and being a good person. Goodness can't be measured by the outward things we do, but by the inward thing we are.

On this matter, C. S. Lewis wrote: "Someone who is not a good tennis player may now and then make a good shot. What you mean by a good player is the man whose eye and muscles and nerves have been so trained by making innumerable good shots that they can now be relied on. They have a certain tone or quality which is there even when he is not playing, just as a mathematician's mind has a certain habit and outlook which is there even when he is not doing mathematics. In the same way a man who perseveres in doing just actions gets in the end a certain quality of character."

It is that inner quality rather than a particular set of actions that Paul refers to in Galatians 5:22 as "goodness," and about which Hugh Latimer noted, "We must first be made good before we can do good."

See also: Romans 7:15–25; Galatians 6:7–10

MARKS OF A CHRISTIAN—GOODNESS

> *He has showed you, O man, what is good. And what does the Lord require of you? To act justly and to love mercy and to walk humbly with your God.*
>
> MICAH 6:8

My first job out of college was working on a small-town newspaper. Every morning I started my day by compiling obituaries for people who had died the night before.

Death notices in little towns are among the most widely read newspaper columns. So I had to do more than call the mortuary to compile a list of survivors and the cause of death. I'd call associates and relatives and friends—they'd often tell me things about the deceased that the mortician didn't know, such as their interests in life, the clubs they had joined, and the good things they had done for the community. In some cases there was little good to be said.

One of the hot movies of the '70s was "Oh, God!" The star, John Denver, received a house call from God, portrayed by George

Burns. Denver was understandably startled, as you would be, too, if God suddenly popped into your home. Once you calmed your jitters and the squeak left your voice, what would you tell God about your life?

Is "goodness" a characteristic you would mention? In the space below, jot down some items you are proudest of about yourself—a list that you'd not want God to leave your home without:

_____

_____

Of course, Christianity is based on grace, not works. There is nothing you can do, no matter how good or great, to talk your way into heaven. However, the values you live by now are the values others will remember you by later. In the end, true goodness never dies.

See also: Romans 2:6–7; Ephesians 2:8–10; 2 Thessalonians 1:11

Religion 101

W
E
E
K

14

MARKS OF A CHRISTIAN—FAITHFULNESS

The fruit of the Spirit is . . . faithfulness.

GALATIANS 5:22

I have been to many weddings where the bride and groom have pledged to remain faithful to each other "until death do us part." Yet within a few short years their relationship is marred by faithlessness.

The change is never a sudden thing. It begins gradually—perhaps when one partner discovers the other gargles wrong, coughs too loud, or squeezes a tube of toothpaste from the top—and then escalates until love is just a memory. This is especially true of couples who think love and faith are things you feel, rather than things you do. When their rosy glow fades, their marriage soon flickers.

If you talk to a husband and wife who have been married a long time, they'll admit they've faced a roller coaster of feelings toward each other—from exuberant highs to gut-wrenching lows. They'll talk about the problems, hardships, and hurts they have experienced together. And then they'll probably smile and say something like: "But it's been worth it."

What do they mean? Simply that the end result of faithfulness outweighs any short-term gain they could have found by ditching love partway. The rewards of long-term love are worth the perseverance and endurance it takes to develop them.

These words *perseverance* and *endurance* appear frequently throughout the Bible where faithfulness is mentioned. Like marriage, your relationship with God will be marked by hardship and heartache. There will be low times when you wake up and don't feel like a Christian . . . and there will be temptations that will sort of blitz your belief.

If your love for God is based on warm feelings, a mere change in mood will destroy the relationship. But where the fruit of faithfulness exists, you'll have your eyes set on the long-term reward and, as C. S. Lewis wrote, "hold onto things your reason once accepted, in spite of your changing moods."

"We'd better get on with it," the writer of Hebrews says (Hebrews 12:1–2 *The Message*). "Strip down, start running—and never quit! No extra spiritual fat, no parasitic sins. Keep your eyes on *Jesus*, who both began and finished this race we're in."

The fruit of faithfulness enables you to complete this difficult race and capture the extravagant rewards God has promised. Get on with it. Just do it.

See also: Proverbs 14:14; Matthew 16:27; 2 John 8–9

MARKS OF A CHRISTIAN— FAITHFULNESS

Do you not know that in a race all the runners run, but only one gets the prize? Run in such a way as to get the prize. Everyone who competes in the games goes into strict training. They do it to get a crown that will not last; but we do it to get a crown that will last forever. Therefore I do not run like a man running aimlessly; I do not fight like a man beating the air. No, I beat my body and make it my slave so that after I have preached to others, I myself will not be disqualified for the prize.

1 CORINTHIANS 9:24–27

Paul never heard of Nikes or Adidas; he probably wasn't even a jogger. Chances are the only exercise he got was running from those who wanted to lynch him. The way he describes his calamities (see 2 Cor. 11:24–33), people were fairly standing in line to do him in.

But he knew enough about track and field to realize that winning was a goal few attained. The rest in the pack have all sorts of reasons for not having won: "It was an off day," "My ankle was

163

sore," "I didn't get enough sleep," "I was slow out of the blocks," "My shoes were bad," "I drank too much water before the race," "My legs just didn't respond."

There are also many reasons Christians give for quitting the race (giving up on God) or slackening their pace (backsliding). Few are faithful to the end. The things that hinder you and hold you back from living the kind of life God wants for you may be many and varied. Your obstacles might be a wrong attitude or bad habit, perhaps a fear of the future, a tendency to lie or lust, or a poor relationship with another person.

Take some time to develop a list of your Big Ten—the ten biggest obstacles that hold you back from running a fast race and being completely faithful to God. Write them down below, using a short phrase or word:

1. _____   6. _____
2. _____   7. _____
3. _____   8. _____
4. _____   9. _____
5. _____   10. _____

If the fruit of faithfulness is missing in your life, your Big Ten is the likely culprit. Talk to God about these regularly, asking him to help you whittle the list down. He's on your side, rooting for you to finish your race.

See also: Galatians 5:7–10; Hebrews 10:36–39, 12:1–3

MARKS OF A CHRISTIAN– GENTLENESS

The fruit of the Spirit is . . . gentleness.

GALATIANS 5:22–23

Gentleness is not something shameful
  Or subordinate
    Or second-best.
It is supreme strength of character—
  Minus the muscle.
Gentleness is being vulnerable and honest—
  Removing your masks and forgetting everything you ever heard
    About "macho" men and Marlboro "manliness."
It says: "Can I help you?"
  And "I'm sorry"
    And "Thanks a million."
Gentleness is admitting you have
  Needs and hurts and fears—
    And is willing to ask for help.
It stands up for the rights of others
  And not for your own.
Gentleness is the unfading beauty of a quiet spirit,
  Or an encouraging word
    Or a kind smile
      Or a good cry.
It is being able to talk openly
  With a member of the opposite sex
    Or to play with a child
      Or to laugh with an adult.
Gentleness soothes the broiling edge of anger
  And hate
    And prejudice
      And pride.
It is strength that grows
  From the inside out.
Gentleness is a velvet-wrapped brick.

See also: Proverbs 15:1–2; 25:15; 1 Peter 3:3–4

MARKS OF A CHRISTIAN— GENTLENESS

Let your gentleness be evident to all.

PHILIPPIANS 4:5

The Bible verses below all describe specific incidents in Christ's life on earth. They present three quick flashes of his character. After each entry, jot down a few notes about what the incident suggests about gentleness, based on Christ's example.

Pass the Kleenex—John 11:32–44

_____

_____

_____

Kid Stuff—Mark 10:13–16

_____

_____

_____

Velvet-Wrapped Brick—John 2:13–16

_____

_____

_____

Some people equate gentleness with weakness. They always have and always will. There were those who probably cringed when Jesus started blubbering at the tomb of Lazarus, and again later when he got choked up about how people in Jerusalem turned their backs on him. Nor did they think it was becoming when he cuddled a bunch of goober-nosed kids. It was only when Jesus raised a little holy hell in the temple that their doubts about his weakness were laid to rest.

Yet even then they mistook the quiet strength of his gentleness for something else.

See also: Ephesians 4:2; 1 Peter 3:13–16

MARKS OF A CHRISTIAN–SELF-CONTROL

The fruit of the Spirit is ... self-control.

GALATIANS 5:22–23

It took more than good intentions and ability for Nancy Swider to make the U.S. Olympic speed skating team and win a world record. Lots of skaters had both and did neither.

It primarily took self-control—the desire to focus every thought on her biggest and best goal and say no to lesser wants. So, late at night when her friends were partying, Nancy would shovel snow from the school track to get in one last set of wind sprints. The next day she would rise with the milkmen for predawn workouts. That's no way to live if you don't care about the Olympics. It's the only way to live if you do.

"To be in good moral condition," wrote Nehru, "requires at least as much training as to be in good physical condition." When you became a Christian, you in effect said yes to God. That's sort of like saying "I do" when you get married. To love your spouse completely, you must forsake all other loves. That means getting rid of certain old pictures in your wallet, scrapping dated love letters, and tossing your little black book.

The same is true of your relationship with God. To love him completely, you must wrench your affections from all that hinders your relationship. To desire his fruit of the Spirit in your life, you must say no to the weeds of the flesh, including such things Paul lists in Galatians 5:19–21: impure thoughts, eagerness for lustful pleasure, hatred and fighting, jealousy and anger, constant effort to get the best for yourself, complaints and criticisms, and the feeling that everyone else is wrong except those in your own little group.

The fruit of self-control is the desire to focus your thoughts on attaining God's biggest and best plans for your life. And once you've made a habit of saying yes to God, saying no to lesser desires is easier. That doesn't mean giving up anything, for "giving up" implies a loss. As Fulton Sheen wrote, "Our Lord did not ask us to give up the things of earth, but to exchange them for better things."

A self-controlled life means you are living an "exchanged" life. Even then, it's no way to live if you don't particularly care what happens on the other side of death. It's the only way to live if you do.

See also: Mark 8:34–38; 1 Thessalonians 5:1–11

MARKS OF A CHRISTIAN—SELF-CONTROL

The highway of the upright avoids evil; he who guards his way guards his soul.

PROVERBS 16:17

I once read a newspaper story about a man from the South whose wife sued him for divorce. The reason? She discovered he was secretly married to two other women, maintained three separate households, three separate families, and three separate jobs in three different states. A salesman, the man would visit one of his families, stay a couple of weeks, and then move on to the next—a pattern he kept up for many years.

Sometimes Christians maintain secret loves. They have pledged their love to God, but in reality they split their affection. They want to be a Christian, but not too Christian. They desire God's will . . . as long as it conforms to their own. They shut the door on sin, but spend the rest of their lives peeking through the keyhole and trying to pick the lock.

As discussed yesterday, the presence of self-control in your life is simply a desire to cultivate God's fruit of the Spirit and to hack away at the roots of the weeds of the flesh. It means not giving in to every desire, whim, and temptation.

The ability to say *No!* to temptation is not some special, mystical, mumbo-jumbo power that belongs solely to those who have memorized Leviticus and can read the Gospels in Greek. It belongs to *you*. Self-control can be evidenced in your life in very practical ways. It means passing up the joint or bottle that is offered you at a party. It means not checking the answers of a friend's test against your own, even when you know they're probably better. It means walking a block out of your way to avoid a magazine rack that tempts you. It means not saying something you have every right to say. And it means waging hand-to-hand combat with the Big Ten you listed earlier this week. Not because you want to appear righteous, but because you realize God's best for your life is better than second, third, or ninth best.

See also: Proverbs 25:28; Titus 2:11–14

GROWING UP

> *Though by this time you ought to be teachers, you need someone to teach you the elementary truths of God's word all over again. You need milk, not solid food! Anyone who lives on milk, being still an infant, is not acquainted with the teaching about righteousness. But solid food is for the mature, who by constant use have trained themselves to distinguish good from evil.*
>
> HEBREWS 5:12–14

When I was a kid, we had a doorway in our house etched with pencil marks. Each year on my birthday, I'd cram my heels against the door frame, stretch my neck as long as possible, and have Mom mark how much I'd grown during the preceding year. Some years there were great spurts. Others, I hardly grew at all. Finally, at 6'-1/2" my growth stopped.

I often think about that doorway. I wonder what it would look like if, instead of my physical growth, it measured my *spiritual* growth. Would the chart mark me as a believer who has "fought the good fight, holding on to faith and a good conscience," or one who has "forsaken my first love."

Some years my growth would have skyrocketed because I was hungry to know more about the Lord and *practice* what I'd learned. I got involved in helping others and saw my friends become Christians. But I'm ashamed to say there would be other years when those growth spurts slowed to an inch or two, and those dark times—signifying periods when I ignored God—when I didn't grow at all.

Thinking back over the years I've been a Christian, I realize you don't just grow old in the Lord. You must also *grow up*. That's what Paul is getting at in the verses in Hebrews. There are some Christians whose spiritual bodies are atrophied and squat. They're still at the Gerber stage, when they should be digesting steak and potatoes.

The result: their spiritual "muscle" is correspondingly misshaped—appearing more like Barbie's than Hulk Hogan's.

How about you? Have you *grown up* and claimed the power that is yours? Or are you living more like a 98-pound weakling—with a spiritual physique to match?

See also: Proverbs 2; Luke 8:5–15; James 1:23–25

NEW LIFE

Forget the former things; do not dwell on the past.
See, I am doing a new thing!

ISAIAH 43:18–19

When I lived in Indiana, my backyard was landscaped with large trees, including several maple and birch, a couple each of apple, cherry, and pear, and one or two oak. With the onset of the cool autumn weather, they all dropped their leaves. Those that didn't fall on their own accord were knocked off by the howling wind, rain, and biting snow of winter. Mother Nature, along about January and February, used brute force to strip the trees to bare-bark skeletons.

Walking through that boneyard backyard one winter, I noticed a few leaves had somehow survived intact—they'd resisted the season's strong-arm tactics and clung tenaciously to branches here and there. The icy winds hadn't blown them off. The snows hadn't knocked them off. The pelting rains hadn't forced them off.

We sometimes have problems like that—problems that cling on and on and on, refusing to let go. Despite what we do to shake them, they persist in plaguing us. It may be a problem with a friend we can't quite clear up, a nagging doubt or inferiority. Maybe it's an ornery boss who won't ease off, or a bad habit that haunts us endlessly. Perhaps it's hassles at home or school that are never-ending. We simply can't get rid of them.

But wait—new life comes! With the onset of spring, the tree's roots extend deeper and pump new life up the trunk to the tip of every branch. Buds appear, pushing the wind-whipped leaves off. At last: every leaf that has clung through winter is pushed off by new buds in the spring.

171

Our problems are the same. Blue days can turn to weeks and months as depression hangs on. We feel doomed by defeats. Our drive is deflated. These problems can't be blown off, shaken off, knocked off. But they are forced off with the help of new life. Christ said, "I am the vine; you are the branches."

He's the new life that surges into our lives, pushing off the old and making room for the new.

See also: John 15:1–8; Romans 6:4; 2 Corinthians 5:17

WEEK

15

LET'S PRETEND

The Lord does not look at the things man looks at. Man looks at the outward appearance, but the Lord looks at the heart.

1 SAMUEL 16:7

The magazine advertisement featured a pretty blonde with a Palm Springs tan and Maybelline looks. Her face was used to hype a leading school of modeling. Beneath the picture was a bold caption: "Be a model . . . or just look like one."

Wouldn't it be strange if that same principle were applied to other things, say Christianity: "Be a Christian . . . or just look like one." What if Jesus had *really* said things such as: "Truly I say to you, if you do not have a fish insignia on your car you cannot be my disciple"; or "Be careful to appear righteous before men, to be seen by them. If you do, you will have a reward from your father in heaven"; or "Whoever wants to become great among you must always wear a pious smile and often say, 'I'll pray for you'"; or "I tell you the truth, unless you act like you're born again, you cannot see the kingdom of God."

Trouble is, we often live as if that's exactly what the Lord did say. We know all the rules of "religiosity" and "churchianity." We know what not to do, or at least what not to get caught doing around certain people. We speak Christianese fluently ("PraiseGawdI'llpray-aboutitLordblessyou!"), and go through the outward motions of *looking* like we think a Christian should and disregard the hard, daily, dirty struggle of *being* a Christian. We woof the woof, but we don't walk the walk.

Though some people might be fooled, God never is. He sees through counterfeit Christianity and knows when we're living by dual standards, with one set of rules for outward behavior and another for our hearts and minds. He knows the #@!*&% stab-in-

174

the-back thoughts we harbor and the jealous, lustful feelings that flood our minds. He knows when we're just pretending to love, pretending to care. He sees straight to the heart. "Before a word is on my tongue you know it completely," David wrote in one of his psalms.

Being a Christian means being concerned about the disparity between how we live and how we look, between what we do and what we say. It helps to know God doesn't just care what we do on Sundays—that we have learned to go to church often enough to be labeled "active" and "faithful." He cares how we live and act the other six days as well. He cares that our Christianity is evidenced in every part of our lives: the mental, social, physical . . . as well as the spiritual.

God wants out of the closet. He wants the freedom to affect every part of our lives. And he wants us to discover the difference between a Sunday school faith and a living, gutsy belief that is more than skin deep.

See also: Psalm 139:4; Romans 12:9–21; 2 Timothy 3:1–5

ONE SOLITARY LIFE

> *The stone the builders rejected has become the capstone.*
>
> **MATTHEW 21:42**

The name of the writer is unknown, but prior to his death he wrote these words about another solitary life:

> Here is a young man who was born in an obscure village, the child of a peasant woman. He grew up in another village. He worked in a carpenter shop until he was thirty, and then for three years he was an itinerant preacher. He never wrote a book. He never held an office. He never owned a home. He never had a family. . . .

He never went to college. He never put his foot inside a big city. He never traveled 200 miles from the place where he was born. He never did one of the things that usually accompany greatness. He had no credentials but himself....

While he was still a young man the tide of public opinion turned against him. His friends ran away. He was turned over to his enemies. He went through the mockery of a trial.

He was nailed to the cross between two thieves. While he was dying, his executioners gambled for the only piece of property he had on earth, and that was his coat. When he was dead he was laid in a borrowed grave through the pity of a friend.

Nineteen centuries wide have come and gone, and today he is the central figure of the human race and the leader of the column of progress....

All the armies that ever marched and all the navies that ever sailed, and all the parliaments that ever sat, and all the kings that ever reigned, put together, have not affected the life of man upon this earth as has that one solitary life.

This man, of course, is Jesus Christ ... who is not just some great, dead leader, but the cornerstone of God's mission of love to earth. "For God so loved the world that he gave his one and only Son, that whoever believes in him shall not perish but have eternal life" (John 3:16).

See also: Philippians 2:5–11

TEAM EFFORT

When Jesus looked up and saw a great crowd coming toward him, he said to Philip, "Where shall we buy bread for these people to eat?" He asked this only to test him, for he already had in mind what he was going to do.

JOHN 6:5–6

The apostle John estimated that there were 5,000 men in that great crowd. But that figure didn't include women and children. So there were probably some 10,000 people milling about—people who had followed Christ's boat around the Sea of Galilee and waited for him to land. They were desperate for his help, and Christ spent the day healing their sick and ministering to their special needs. As nightfall approached, another more basic need arose: The people had nothing to eat. And all of the Burger Kings were closed.

It was at this point Christ approached Philip. "Where shall we buy burgers for these people to eat?" Jesus asked. The question seemed absurd. Didn't Christ know the situation was hopeless?

"Eight months' wages would not buy enough Whoppers for each one to have a bite," Philip quickly responded. Other disciples rallied around Philip by urging Christ to "send the crowds away." *Come on, Jesus. Be serious. What you ask is crazy. Utterly impossible!*

Christ probably felt a twinge of sadness in his heart. The Bible says Jesus asked Philip the question simply as a test, *for he already had in mind what he was going to do.* The question was a way of asking, "Philip, will you trust me with this seemingly impossible situation? Will you refuse to trust your own understanding and allow me to work out a solution?"

That's the same question you face every day in myriad ways. Perhaps your family is on the rocks, or maybe there's a situation at school that seems hopeless. Your "impossibility" might concern your future, a bad habit you've been unable to kick, or a serious problem with a friend. Regardless of the specifics, the question Christ raised with Philip is unchanging: *"What are we going to do?"* Jesus wants to work with you in a team effort.

In the story above, Christ already had a plan worked out. He knew the solution. And he always does. What may seem impossible to you is possible to God.

See also: Proverbs 3:5–6; Matthew 19:26

JESUS OF CHINA

I have set you an example that you should do as I have done for you.

JOHN 13:15

One of the United States' earliest missionaries to China, Henry Poppen, made an extended trek to a remote village. Though he'd lived in that country for some forty years, he knew of no Christian who had ever visited the secluded little town with its unadorned huts and simple people.

Upon his arrival, the villagers listened patiently as he tried to explain who Jesus was. He talked about Christ's gentleness, his truthfulness, his all-encompassing love. The villagers nodded their heads and smiled. Some had moist eyes.

He described how Jesus bore no grudges when wronged, how he lived for what he could give rather than get. He spoke about how Christ was selfless to the point of death.

The grizzled old villagers glanced back and forth with knowing eyes. Finally, one of them spoke. "We know this man. Your 'Jesus' lived here."

Dr. Poppen smiled, but shook his head. Feeling there was some misunderstanding, he explained that Christ had actually lived many thousands of miles away.

"No, no. He lived and died right here," the old, wrinkled villager insisted. Rising to his feet, he pointed off in the distance down a rutted dirt path. "Follow me, I'll show you his grave."

Dr. Poppen shrugged his shoulders and followed. He trudged behind the pack of men and women as they guided him away from the huts to a Chinese cemetery. There they stopped at a headstone carved with the name of a Christian medical missionary— a man who felt God had led him to that secluded corner of the world. He had lived and died there—his existence unknown even to other missionaries. Yet he was so Christlike that Jesus of Nazareth was mistaken for "Jesus" of China.

Every Christian is a missionary—God's representative—in his or her own corner of the world. In *your* school, *your* home, *your* job, you'll meet people no other Christian can.

That's why Christ said his life is an example for you. By following it and being faithful to the pattern, others are bound to see Christ in you . . . and perhaps to even mistake you for the real thing.

See also: 2 Corinthians 5:20; Philippians 2:5–8; 1 Timothy 1:15–16

THE SIXTH MAN

Greater love has no one than this, that he lay down his life for his friends.

JOHN 15:13

Flight 90 began like any other flight: the dash down the runway, the gentle lurch skyward, the stewardess saying something about the location of exits. Sitting quietly in the rear, a balding man in his 50s fingered his extravagant mustache and stared out the 737's window at the bite of winter. The heavy snowfall obscured vision of the frozen Washington, D.C., landscape below.

Suddenly, tragedy struck. The Florida-bound plane with 74 passengers skidded across a traffic-clogged bridge. Cars were sheared in half. Then the jet quickly sank beneath the ice-clogged Potomac River.

When a rescue helicopter arrived, only six passengers were visible. As they floundered in the icy water, losing their grip on life, the helicopter dangled a life preserver to the man with the mustache. But each time the ring was lowered, the man passed it to someone else who was then shuttled safely to shore. He waved the ring off five times. When the helicopter finally returned for him, the man had disappeared to his death ... anonymously and selflessly, known only as "the sixth man."

A hero? Yes. A Christian? No one knows. But in his last minutes of life he faced death with charity and gave his life so others might live.

I sometimes wonder if I would have done the same. Probably not. And then I think, Is there anyone I'd die for, *really*, if the choice was set before me? My parents? Well, they're kind of old and ... My brother or sister? We've never really been too close ... My best friend? Too flippant....

In the end, I'd want to be absolutely sure the person I swapped my life for was *worth* it — I might consider giving up my life if the individual was some kind of cross between Einstein and Billy Graham, but even then ...

Compared to the Bible's standards (and to "the sixth man's"), my love and selflessness are pretty puny. And then I stop and think about how Christ gave his life for me. By my standards I wouldn't be *worth* dying for. But by God's standards, everyone was worth dying for.

His evaluation was a radical valuation. The world still hasn't gotten over it.

See also: Romans 5:6–8; Mark 8:34–38

⸬⸬⸬

HOMEWARD BOUND

Even to your old age and gray hairs I am he, I am he who will sustain you. I have made you and I will carry you.

ISAIAH 46:4

The first Saturday of each month, I'd meet Grandpa on the Ocean Beach pier. We'd each bring a fishing pole, tackle box, and bucket for any fish we might catch. He always razzed me that he'd catch the bigger fish, though we both seldom caught anything but seaweed. So on the way home, we'd stop and buy some fresh bass fillets. Grandma always thought they were fish we'd caught ourselves, which made Grandpa smile and wink.

He was a simple man. He liked the quiet solitude he found while fishing, he liked to walk in the woods, he liked to read his Bible, and he seldom missed church on Sunday. He was at home there, and tried to arrive early so he could shake hands with all of his friends.

Things changed somewhat when Grandpa had a stroke and lost most of his hearing. Sometimes he'd be out walking and have what he'd call a "spell." Something in his head would click, and he'd crumple unconscious to the ground.

After that point, he still made it to church sometimes, and would shake hands all around. He'd turn his hearing aid up until it buzzed, but even then I don't think he heard much of the sermon. Yet he'd sit in his regular spot three pews from the front, his gentle face shining with the joy of one who's made his peace with God.

As years passed, I grew up and moved away. And Grandpa just grew older. I got letters from him often—letters that talked about how he enjoyed watching the birds or fixing breakfast for Grandma, or how the Lord was as natural to him as his next breath. But his handwriting got shaky, and he began having more "spells." We both knew his home-going was drawing near, and that saddened me. But the thought didn't bother him. He said, smiling, that it would be like getting in an old fishing boat and crossing from one shore to another—and greeting the Lord face-to-face on the other side.

Most people think growing old and dying are life's greatest tragedies. To them, Grandpa would say, "Humbug!" And he would stamp his foot when saying it. And then he'd point out, as did Melville, that life is a voyage that's homeward bound.

See also: John 14:2; 1 Thessalonians 4:13–18

POINTS TO PONDER–LIFE AND DEATH

Whoever finds his life will lose it, and whoever loses his life for my sake will find it.

MATTHEW 10:39

Life is not lost by dying; life is lost minute by minute, day by dragging day, in all the thousand small uncaring ways.

STEPHEN VINCENT BENÉT

It matters not how long you live, but how well.

PUBLILIUS SYRUS

Religion can offer a man a burial service, but Christ offers every man new, abundant and everlasting life.

WILMA REED

Not, how did he die? But, how did he live?
Not, what did he gain? But, what did he give?
These are the merits to measure the worth
Of a man as man, regardless of birth.
Not, what was his station? But, had he a heart?
And how did he play his God-given part?
Was he ever ready with word or good cheer
To bring a smile, to banish a tear?
Not, what was his church? Nor, what was his creed?
But, had he befriended those really in need?

Not, what did the sketch in the newspaper say?
But, how many were sorry when he passed away?

UNKNOWN

We go to the grave of a friend, saying, "A man is dead." But angels throng about him, saying, "A man is born."

GOTTHOLD

Those who live in the Lord never see each other for the last time.

GERMAN SAYING

Creative life is always on the yonder side of convention.

C. G. JUNG

I believe in life after birth.

UNKNOWN

Have you wept at anything during the past year? Has your heart beat faster at the sight of young beauty? Have you thought seriously about the fact that someday you are going to die? More often than not do you really listen when people are speaking to you instead of just waiting for your turn to speak? Is there anybody you know in whose place, if one of you had to suffer great pain, you would volunteer yourself? If your answer to all or most of these questions is No, the chances are that you're dead.

FREDERICK BUECHNER

To fear love is to fear life, and those who fear life are already three parts dead.

BERTRAND RUSSELL

Death is more universal than life; everyone dies but not everyone lives.

A. SACHS

183

Life is like a cash register, in that every account, every thought, every deed, like every sale, is registered and recorded.

FULTON J. SHEEN

Take care of your life; and the Lord will take care of your death.

GEORGE WHITEFIELD

The waters are rising but I am not sinking.

CATHERINE BOOTH (LAST WORDS)

Death: to stop sinning suddenly.

ELBERT HUBBARD

[Some say] that death ought not to be final, that there ought to be a second chance. I believe that if a million chances were likely to do good, they would be given. But a master often knows, when boys and parents do not, that it is really useless to send a boy in for a certain examination again. Finality must come sometime, and it does not require a very robust faith to believe that omniscience knows when.

C. S. LEWIS

Life can only be understood backward; it must be lived forward.

SOREN KIERKEGAARD

See also: Job 1:21; Matthew 7:13–14; John 10:10; 1 Corinthians 15:50–55; Revelation 21:1–4

TRUE LOVE

> *The commandments, "Do not commit adultery,"*
> *"Do not murder," "Do not steal," "Do not covet," and*
> *whatever other commandment there may be, are summed*
> *up in this one rule: "Love your neighbor as yourself."*
>
> ROMANS 13:9

One of the nonfiction bestsellers a few years ago was a book called *Looking Out for Number One*. I didn't buy it because, rightly or wrongly, I've always been *very* good at looking out for myself and figured I didn't need additional help. For example:

I pamper myself. My favorite way to pamper myself is to do what I most enjoy—like running barefoot through mud, making faces in the mirror, and swishing Jell-O in my teeth. I also pamper myself by guzzling root beer on a hot day, going to a movie when I'm bored, and changing my socks when they smell.

I protect myself. When I head to the beach, I grease up with sun block. I also play it safe by wearing gloves in the snow, carrying a spare tire in my trunk, and by staying away from those who sneeze. Friends, books, and a portable CD player protect me from loneliness.

I challenge myself. I challenge myself by always trying to run a faster mile, by looking at stars through a telescope, or a drop of puddle water through a microscope. Perhaps my biggest challenge is just trying to be myself.

I honor myself. When I've done something well, I honor myself by broadcasting my accomplishment. "Hey, I just sold another magazine article!" I'll shout to a friend across the grocery store aisle. And when the check comes in the mail, the first dollar is spent on myself to celebrate my success.

I accept myself. I don't like the way I sound on a tape recorder and I don't like my knobby bird legs. But I've learned to accept what I cannot change. I know I will never be a good spellur or the life of a party. But that's OK—I wouldn't be *me* otherwise.

If it sounds like I think of myself a lot it's because I do. I pamper, protect, challenge, honor, and accept myself for one reason: *I love myself.* There's nothing wrong with that. God doesn't want me to love myself any less. He just wants me to love others the same way.

See also: Luke 10:25–37; John 13:34–35; 1 John 3:11–18

LASTING MEMORIES

Whatever you do, whether in word or deed, do it all in the name of the Lord Jesus.

COLOSSIANS 3:17

I was visiting a town I'd never been in before and stopped for a pizza. Suddenly I heard someone calling my name from the far side of the restaurant. It was Tony, a high school friend whom I'd not seen in years. I joined him for dinner, and for the next couple of hours we talked of "the good old days."

"Remember Harry?" Tony said late in the evening. I nodded with a smile. Everyone always used to make fun of Harry. Then, laughing hard, he described an impersonation of Harry I'd done one day in speech class when the teacher stepped out. I tried hard, but couldn't remember the incident.

"I'll never forget it," said Tony, nearly in hysterics by that time. "I remember it every time I think of you."

Later that night I pondered what Tony had said. A scene I couldn't even recall was printed indelibly in his mind. He remembered it as being funny. But the laughs were all at Harry's expense.

I would like to have been remembered in other, kinder ways: the weekends I spent working with Mexican orphans, the day I took a retarded girl on a wheelchair stroll to the 7–11 store, the time I tutored a friend all night in English. But it was my mimicry of Harry's duck walk and stutter that Tony best remembered.

The role I play in the memories of others is bothersome, because their minds, like security cameras, record everything. What they remember about me is something I cannot control. *Or can I?*

Thinking of this incident with Tony, I've often stopped myself just as I'm getting ready to lash out at somebody in anger. I've caught myself on the verge of making a crude comment, excusing my behavior to my family, or telling a lie. Knowing that my every action and comment can be recorded in the mind's camera of others, I try harder to guard my words and behavior.

When the camera clicks on, I want only my best side to show.

See also: Proverbs 29:11; James 3:3–12

THE QUICK FIX

Consider it pure joy, my brothers, whenever you face trials of many kinds, because you know that the testing of your faith develops perseverance. Perseverance must finish its work so that you may be mature and complete, not lacking anything.

JAMES 1:2–4

When you grow up in a society that pioneered such things as instant pudding, minute rice, freeways, one-step cameras, and fast-food restaurants, waiting does not come easy. If you must wait longer than 30 seconds for a Big Mac, you start glancing at your watch, wondering if the zit-faced cook isn't missing half his brain. And when you later develop indigestion, you grab an instant solution from the nearest medicine chest.

In this "aspirin age" of ours, we've also come to expect instant solutions to our personal pressures and daily trials. We don't want a timely struggle with our problems—we'd prefer to catapult over them. We want to smile and feel happy and say "Praise the

Lord!" a lot. So we attend all kinds of Bible studies, victory rallies, youth camps, super Sunday seminars, and revival meetings to discover the spiritual key and that hidden verse that will help us combat "what's wrong" in our lives.

Yet, what's wrong is that we want answers—NOW! And if our youth pastor or minister can't provide them, we'll hop to another church to get the spiritual "fix" that hopefully—for another hour, day, or week—will numb the panic and pressure we feel about school, work, a personal relationship, our future, or our families.

The daily frustrations we want off our backs are the very things James says we not only ought to endure, but endure *joyfully*. The joy comes from knowing the difficulties we face help us grow up spiritually. In other words, negative experiences can produce positive results. The lives of Joseph, Sarah, Job, Daniel, and Paul all attest to this.

I like to think of these experiences as pearls. Pearls don't just happen. To begin with, a grain of sand imbeds itself in the soft inner folds of an oyster, which in turn soothes the irritant with a rich body fluid. In time, and plenty of it, that fluid forms a smooth, hard surface—a pearl.

And so it is with us: God is at work in our lives, turning our biggest irritants into priceless, one-of-a-kind gems. It's a timely process that can't be rushed.

See also: Romans 5:3–5; Philippians 1:4–6

GO THE DISTANCE

Pursue righteousness, godliness, faith, love, endurance and gentleness. Fight the good fight of the faith.

1 TIMOTHY 6:11–12

One of the most successful movies of all time was the original *Rocky*—the roaches-to-riches story of an untested Philadelphia brawler who was given a chance to box the world champion. It was all a public relations gimmick hatched by the champ hitman, Apollo Creed.

A cute idea, Rocky's friends agreed. But they also agreed the odds against their "Italian Stallion" were overwhelming. The Creed would make hamburger of him. Rocky didn't doubt it would be a tough fight—he simply wanted to complete the 15 grueling rounds, to remain standing at the final bell. In his words, he wanted to "go the distance."

In a fight of another sort—a bout without satin trunks and Everlast gloves—the apostle Paul faced similar staggering odds. His was a spiritual battle, yet he maintained the same goal of "going the distance." If you think Rocky had it tough, read 2 Corinthians 11:24–33. It's Paul's account of the beatings, whippings, stonings, shipwrecks, imprisonments, and threats he faced in his "fight of the faith." Yet he endured and persevered through every trial, temptation, discouragement and despair.

At the end of his life he could write: "I'm about to die, my life an offering on God's altar. This is the only race worth running. I've run hard right to the finish, believed all the way. All that's left now is the shouting—God's applause! Depend on it, he's an honest judge. He'll do right not only by me, but by everyone eager for his coming" (2 Tim. 4:6–8, *The Message*).

In the "fight of the faith," the odds sometimes seem staggering. You face temptations daily that blitz your belief. You face moral decisions that others never have to consider. Yet the Bible indicates an eternal prize awaits those who remain faithful to the final bell.

It's one thing to join the fight for a time, and then quit. It's quite another to go the distance and finish it.

See also: 1 Corinthians 9:24–27; 1 Timothy 4:7–8; 2 John 8–9

FAITH IS A VERB

Faith by itself, if it is not accompanied by action, is dead.

JAMES 2:17

Charles Blondin is credited with having crossed Niagara Falls several times—on a 1,100-foot tightrope, 160 dizzying feet above the thundering water. His high-wire feats often included theatrical variations, such as walking on stilts or pushing a wheelbarrow. He'd even pause to stand on his head, turn a backward somersault, balance atop a chair, or cook an omelette!

One day in 1860, Blondin was again preparing to cross the famous falls. He turned to the huge crowd and asked if they believed he could cross without falling. They shouted their assent. He asked if they believed he could do it carrying another person on his back. Again the crowd roared. But when Blondin asked a man standing nearby to volunteer, the man refused.

Had the man believed, I mean *really* believed, his faith would have prompted him to climb atop Blondin's back. True faith is more than just mental assent or verbal agreement. It involves action.

The same is true, James writes, of those who profess to believe in Christ. Faith is dead if it's not accompanied by action.

Put your faith to the test by getting involved in people's lives. Don't just pray for others; roll up your sleeves and help them. Anyone can say they believe. But how many are willing, for example, to spend time with the unpopular kid at school whom others ignore?

Your faith and love for God ought to motivate you to love others—actively and practically. Faith like that speaks louder than words.

See also: Genesis 15:1–6; Mark 9:14–24

HOLDING OUT

We live by faith, not by sight.

2 CORINTHIANS 5:7

Those who like baseball will never forget the 1994 season. It was the year players went on strike. TV sets were quiet. There was no World Series. Stadiums were as still as a small-town street after midnight. Season tickets had all been sold, but games were canceled because the players were holding out. They wanted more money, more benefits, more guarantees.

When it comes to holding out on God, most of us are pros. We want to play by our rules come hell or high water. Back in high school when I first sensed a need for God, I did a lot of bargaining. It was June, during the three-month summer siesta. I more or less told God I wanted to wait until September to become a Christian. Summers were too much fun to be wrecked by going to church, reading a Bible, and worrying about things like drinking and going to the wrong parties. Trouble is, God *waited*. And I had my most miserable summer ever.

People hold out on God in other, different ways. They want guarantees. They'll do what God wants, *if* . . . You know, *if* God gets them the job they want, *if* God heals their mom's cancer, *if* God allows them to fall in love, *if* God gets them accepted to the right college, *if* God lets them be a cheerleader or baseball team all-star. The list is a mile long.

But we've got it all wrong. God doesn't promise us fail-safe, risk-free Christianity. He doesn't assure us things will work out like in the movies, with everyone living happily ever after. He doesn't guarantee us immunity from hurt and hardship. There are no guarantees other than the fact that he'll be our God if we'll be his people.

We want promises, but God wants faith. Sure, there are risks. But faith takes the risks, without knowing where it is being led. That's because faith loves and follows—no strings attached—the one who leads: Jesus Christ.

You can think of it as taking a trip without maps. Or you can think of it as a true and absolute adventure.

See also: Hebrews 11

POINTS TO PONDER—FAITH

> ***Faith is being sure of what we hope for and certain of what we do not see.***
>
> **HEBREWS 11:1**

I believe in the sun, even when it is not shining; I believe in love even when I feel it not; I believe in God, even when he is silent.

ANONYMOUS

I prayed for faith and thought that some day faith would come down and strike me like lightning. But faith did not seem to come. One day I read in the 10th chapter of Romans, "Faith cometh by hearing, and hearing by the Word of God." I had up to this time closed my Bible and prayed for faith. I now opened my Bible and began to study, and faith has been growing ever since.

D. L. MOODY

Life has no question that faith cannot answer.

THOMAS L. JOHNS

Faith is love taking the form of aspiration.

WILLIAM ELLERY CHANNING

I always prefer to believe the best of everybody—it saves so much trouble.

RUDYARD KIPLING

God made the moon as well as the sun: and when he does not see fit to grant us the sunlight, he means us to guide our steps as well as we can by moonlight.

RICHARD WHATELY

Faith makes things possible—it does not make them easy.

ANONYMOUS

The life of faith is not a life of mounting up with wings, but a life of walking and not fainting.... Faith never knows where it is being led, but it loves and knows the one who is leading.

OSWALD CHAMBERS

Never put a question mark where God has put a period.

JOHN R. RICE

I back the scent of life
Against its stink.
That's what faith works out at
Finally.

G. A. STUDDERT KENNEDY

Never, never pin your whole faith on any human being: not if he is the best and wisest in the whole world. There are lots of nice things you can do with sand; but do not try building a house on it.

C. S. LEWIS

Faith is not being sure where you're going but going anyway. A journey without maps.

FREDERICK BUECHNER

Faith is not believing that God *can*, but that God *will!*

ABRAHAM LINCOLN

Don't be afraid to take a big step if one is indicated. You can't cross a chasm in two small jumps.

DAVID LLOYD GEORGE

Faith is not an effort, a striving, a ceaseless seeking, as so many earnest souls suppose, but rather a letting go, an abandonment, an abiding rest in God that nothing, not even the soul's short-comings, can disturb.

ANONYMOUS

Faith is an inner conviction of being overwhelmed by God.

GUSTAF AULÉ

See also: Matthew 17:20; Romans 10:17; Ephesians 2:8; Hebrews 11

WEEK

17

WHO IS HE?

A very large crowd spread their cloaks on the road, while others cut branches from the trees and spread them on the road. The crowds that went ahead of him and those that followed shouted, "Hosanna to the Son of David!" "Blessed is he who comes in the name of the Lord!" "Hosanna in the highest!"

When Jesus entered Jerusalem, the whole city was stirred and asked, "Who is this?"

MATTHEW 21:8–10

I was at New York's Kennedy airport one evening when a crowd of people swarmed the gate of an approaching 747. Most had their cameras cocked and were bouncing nervously on their feet.

Suddenly, a popular rock musician stepped through the door. Pandemonium broke loose. Flashes exploded. Girls elbowed closer. And everyone battled for autographs.

I was standing near an elderly lady, who had stopped out of curiosity. She wore a puzzled look and tapped me on the shoulder. "Excuse me," she said, "but who is that?"

A similar thing happened when Jesus entered Jerusalem on Palm Sunday, just five days before his death. A huge crowd had gathered, ensuring his arrival into the grand capital city would never be forgotten. There was much commotion and shouting among those who knew about Jesus, his miracles and claims. The fuss was so great, Matthew wrote, that the whole city was stirred into frenzy. Yet there were many, he noted, who scratched their heads and asked those standing nearby, "Pardon me, but who's the guy on the donkey?"

They were puzzled about Jesus of Nazareth. Could he possibly be the one and only Son of God as he claimed? Had God actually stepped out of the shadows, so to speak, and shown his face? The Old Testament forecast it. And everyone knew if you read it there, it *had* to be true. But still, how could it be? It didn't make sense that the homeless, jobless son of two hick Jews could be who he claimed.

As C. S. Lewis wrote on this matter: "A man who was merely a man and said the sort of things Jesus said wouldn't be a great moral teacher. He's either be a lunatic—on a level with a man who says he's a poached egg—or else he'd be the devil of hell. You must make your choice. Either this man was, and is, the son of God, or else a madman or something worse."

Questions about Christ's identity haven't changed much in 2,000 years. Either he was a full-tilt crazy with the asylum key, or he carried the key to unlock the entire universe. The choice is yours: Kook of kooks or King of kings.

See also: Joshua 24:14–18; Matthew 16:13–16

OLD CHARLIE

I am just like you before God; I too have been taken from clay.

JOB 33:6

As I walked past Old Charlie's house on the way home from school, I spotted him on the porch swing, just staring away his time. Normally I wouldn't have bothered with him. After all, we had nothing in common; sixty years separated us. He'd always seemed like a leftover relic from some long-ago age.

But my grandma had died just a few weeks before, and I got to thinking that he probably wasn't too many steps from the grave himself. So I threw my hand in the air and waved. "How ya doing, Charlie?" I shouted.

He grunted something I couldn't hear. I had time to kill, so I crossed his lawn and stepped up on the porch. I stood around for a few minutes, wondering how you talk to an old man. Finally, not knowing what else to say, I asked if he was married.

"Naw. The wife's been gone now twenty years." He started tugging on his collar and looking into the sky as if he were trying to spot Jupiter. "But I'm thinking of getting hitched again," he said, looking as nervous to me as I probably looked to him.

"Got a girlfriend, eh, Charlie?"

"Aw, it's hardly worth talking about. Every time I bring the subject up, my family makes a big deal about my age. You'd think I'm old enough to make my own decisions, but they treat me like a kid."

"Things aren't much better around my place," I joked, relaxing a bit. Somehow we got talking about other things: my studies, my job hunt (my age was always a problem), football, and how it looked like the Chargers would finally make the Super Bowl.

"I'd of bought me a season pass if I had the money," he said. "But I'd of needed a job, and nobody wants someone *my* age."

Suddenly it struck me. "You know, the thing about you, Charlie, is . . . well, you're just like me."

That night as I lay in bed, I wondered how many other people I'd shut out of my life—simply because they didn't look, talk, or dress like me. How many other *Charlies* had I excluded?

See also: Isaiah 35:3–4; Matthew 5:46–47; Romans 12:16; 1 Corinthians 13:4–7

⁂⁂⁂

PRESERVE AND SEASON

You are the salt of the earth.

MATTHEW 5:13

If Christ were speaking today to a contemporary audience, he might not have used salt as a metaphor to describe the intended relationship between Christians and the rest of the world. Instead, he might have said, "You are the Kenmore refrigerator of the world."

Two thousand years ago, salt served the same basic purpose as refrigeration does today. It was a preservative—a means to maintain freshness and hinder decay. Meats, fish, and poultry were either rubbed carefully with salt or allowed to soak in a brine solution to ward off the natural rotting process.

Our purpose as Christians should be to penetrate the non-Christian community with the message of God's love and saving power, and thereby ward off spiritual decay. We shouldn't stand apart from the world and piously exclaim, "Things sure are a mess these days. The divorce rate is up, the crime rate is up, the suicide rate is up." What's so surprising about that, anyway? After all, Christ indicates that people without God are like meat without salt. There is a natural rotting process. So let's please pass the salt . . . quickly!

Christ goes on to warn that salt that's lost its saltiness is good for nothing, except to be thrown out and trampled. Tough words, and rightly so. God is a jealous God. He paid an immeasurable price for our salvation by sending his only Son to the cross. If we habitually and purposefully sin, we ignore God's sacrifice. We also deny him the opportunity to use our lives to penetrate, preserve, and season the lives of non-Christians with whom we have daily contact.

If we're truly salt, we need to be about God's business. We need to get out of the salt shaker.

See also: Matthew 5:14–16; 28:18–20; Colossians 3:1–17

AGE-OLD CONCERNS

Don't let anyone look down on you because you are young, but set an example for the believers in speech, in life, in love, in faith and in purity.

1 TIMOTHY 4:12

You haven't seen the fat cousin of your mom's in many years. "Last time I saw you," she grins, "you could run under the breadboard. And now look at my Little Chrissy," she says, giving your cheek a playful pinch.

Your coach glares down at you. "You call that a push-up?" he barks. "I want to see your chest BOUNCE. Do it again! ONE ... TWO ... Faster! ... THREE ... FOUR ... Work off that baby fat! ... FIVE ... SIX ..."

You approach your dad cautiously. All you want is to borrow a few bucks for your first razor. Admittedly, you're a "late bloomer." But you're not prepared for his response. "Stand in the light," he says, trying to stifle a laugh. "I'll get that whisker with the tweezers."

Adults probably don't mean much by such comments, but their remarks can eat at your insides for days and reinforce the myriad anxieties and insecurities you already have. At a time when you feel very grown-up and are having to make sweeping decisions about your future (College? Career? Marriage?), you're constantly belittled and reminded of your youth.

Timothy was in a similar position. It's not known how old he was when Paul told him, "Don't let anyone look down on you because you are young," but he was young enough that Paul elsewhere refers to him as "son." And he was young enough to be chastised about his age—otherwise Paul wouldn't have brought the subject up. Perhaps Timothy had somehow communicated that he felt young and inexperienced—that he'd be more effective for the Lord if he was a little older.

Whatever the situation was, Paul told him that his actions, his quality of life, and everyday, practical godliness would speak louder than his age. In other words, he was saying Timothy's *spiritual* maturity mattered more than his *physical* maturity.

That's the same message God conveyed to Jeremiah when the young prophet complained of being too young to do what God had in mind for him. "Do not say, 'I am only a child' ... for I am with you," the Lord said. And his message is the same today.

If you feel hindered by your age or limited talents, remember that these are not concerns of God's. He can use your life in very big, extraordinary ways if you're willing to trust him in very ordinary ways each and every day of your life ... *for he is with you.*

See also: Jeremiah 1:4–10; Romans 8:31; Ephesians 4:10–16; 1 Peter 2:1–3

LIFE IN THE FAST LANE

Come near to God and he will come near to you. Wash your hands, you sinners, and purify your hearts, you double-minded.

JAMES 4:8

Gregg had been active in church—one of the leader types. But after graduation he started working for his father in a lucrative family business, and I seldom saw him again. I don't know what he made, but it was big bucks. He paid cash for a fire-truck-red Mustang and drove it off the lot one Saturday.

On Friday nights he party-hopped until 3:00 a.m. and once confided, "Mike, that was some par-tee! Two girls for every guy, and enough booze to float a boat in!" At one of the parties he met a flight attendant, and a few months later she moved into his park-front condo.

I bumped into him once at the mall and asked how things were.

"Hey, great! Got a new girl, and just bought a new ski boat."

"You sound pretty happy."

The comment stopped him cold. He shifted on his feet and looked down. "Yeah, I suppose." For some reason he started talking, and eventually got around to saying he wanted to get back with God and how he felt *old* at twenty-two. "Everyone thinks I've got it great, but they don't really know ..."

As Gregg talked, I got to thinking about a story I once heard about how some hunters in South America catch monkeys. They drill a small hole in a coconut, drain the milk, and scrape out the meat. Then they drop in a piece of candy and chain it to a tree.

A monkey, I was told, is curious enough that it will stick its hand through the hole and grab the candy. But its clenched fist is too big for the hole. The only way to release its hand is to let go of the candy. Trouble is, a monkey is too greedy for that. It'll scream all day trying to bash the coconut. It's doomed because it won't make the choice to give up the sweet. Eventually a hunter will wander by, brain the monkey, and take it home to barbecue.

Gregg had the potential to do something decent with his life and to find true contentment. But there were some things he needed to let go of first.

See also: Isaiah 1:18; 2 Corinthians 7:1; Ephesians 4:17–24

BE PREPARED

Why do you stand here looking into the sky? This same Jesus, who has been taken from you into heaven, will come back in the same way you have seen him go into heaven.

ACTS 1:11

From the time I became a Christian in high school and heard someone pray, "Come soon, Lord Jesus," I've always been excited about the Second Coming. The very thought is staggering: a person who died some 2,000 years ago is still alive ... and will return to earth!

When will it happen? Tomorrow? Next month? In five years? There are some honest disagreements among sincere Bible scholars about the timing of Christ's homecoming. Some very popular books have been written on the subject, complete with charts, diagrams and predictions to make everything seem precise. Other authors interpret biblical prophecy differently. The dates they've circled in red are not the same.

But the Bible is clear about one thing: "No one knows about that day or hour, not even the angels in heaven, nor the Son, but only the Father.... Therefore keep watch, because you do not know on what day your Lord will come (Matt. 24:36, 42).

Why will it happen? There are two basic reasons why the return trip will be made. First, Christ will come to judge sin and to honor faithfulness. Some people think they can get away with anything, but we are all accountable for our sin. When Christ returns, "All the nations will be gathered before him, and he will separate the people one from another as a shepherd separates the sheep from the goats.... Then they will go away to eternal punishment, but the righteous to eternal life" (Matt. 25:32, 46). In other words, the choices we make on earth are binding in eternity.

Second, Christ will come to rule. The world is currently in rebellion against God, with the rebel leader being Satan himself. But that will all change when Christ returns! As promised in Revelation 11:15, "The kingdom of the world has become the kingdom of our Lord and of his Christ, and he will reign for ever and ever."

All of this talk about judging and reigning is, of course, very true. But it sounds rather formal and stiff. I'm sure that much of the reasoning behind Christ's Second Coming is simply his desire to return to his old stomping grounds to be with old friends and loved ones. It's a homecoming you won't want to miss!

See also: 1 Thessalonians 4:13–5:11

POINTS TO PONDER–HEAVEN

Our citizenship is in heaven.

PHILIPPIANS 3:20

To believe in heaven is not to run away from life; it is to run toward it.

JOSEPH D. BLINCO

Heaven will be the perfection we have always longed for. All the things that made earth unlovely and tragic will be absent in heaven. There will be no night, no death, no disease, no sorrow, no tears, no ignorance, no disappointment, no war. It will be filled with health, vigor, virility, knowledge, happiness, worship, love and perfection.

BILLY GRAHAM

A man's reach should exceed his grasp,
Or what's a heaven for?

ROBERT BROWNING

If I find in myself a desire which no experience in this world can satisfy, the most probable explanation is that I was made for another world.

C. S. LEWIS

What a pity the only way to heaven is in a hearse.

STANISLAW J. LEC

To be in hell is to drift; to be in heaven is to steer.

GEORGE BERNARD SHAW

A continual looking forward to the eternal world is not a form of escapism or wishful thinking, but one of the things a Christian is meant to do. It does not mean that we are to leave the present world as it is. If you read history, you will find that the Christians who did the most for the present world were just those who thought most of the next.

C. S. LEWIS

Religion can offer a person a burial service, but Christ offers every person new, abundant and everlasting life.

WILMA REED

Life's a voyage that's homeward bound.

HERMAN MELVILLE

There is nothing in the world of which I feel so certain. I have no idea what it will be like, and I am glad that I have not, as I am sure it would be wrong. I do not want it for myself as mere continuance, but I want it for my understanding of life. And moreover "God is love" appears to me nonsense in view of the world he has made, if there is no other.

WILLIAM TEMPLE

Take care of your life; and the Lord will take care of your death.

GEORGE WHITEFIELD

Faith is the Christian's foundation, hope is his anchor, death is his harbor, Christ is his pilot and heaven is his country.

JEREMY TAYLOR

When you speak of heaven let your face light up. When you speak of hell—well, then your everyday face will do.

CHARLES H. SPURGEON

A good many people will see little heaven hereafter if they do not begin to look for more of heaven now.

RICHARD MONTAGUE

See also: Isaiah 65:17–25; John 14:1–6

WEEK

18

ONE DAY AT A TIME

This is the day the Lord has made; let us rejoice and be glad in it.

PSALM 118:24

Just for today I will try not to fret about yesterday's "F" in math or worry about tomorrow's Spanish test. I will banish anxiety and forget past mistakes. I will discover God's will for my life one day at a time.

Just for today I will not try to appear perfectly packaged. I will feel free to cry, to doubt, to express my fears, to laugh till I hurt. I will think less about the mirror and about pleasing people and more about pleasing God.

Just for today I will be a good listener—no strings attached. I will comfort others . . . and keep my mouth shut. I will love others for *who* they are (unique creations of God) rather than for *what* they are (good-looking, funny, rich). I will do something nice for my parents.

Just for today I will take time to create a memory. I will *make* someone a birthday card instead of buying a Hallmark. I will take a walk at sunset. I will pick a flower, talk to a child, read an entire book in the Bible, smile at a teacher, take a bubble bath, greet a stranger. I will take off my watch.

Just for today I will try to be scrupulously honest. I will be literal about right and wrong. I won't sneak into the store express lane with twelve items when the sign says "ten items or less." I will drive *under* the speed limit.

Just for today I will trust God for the "impossible": a friendship healed, a bad memory erased, a sin forgiven, a family reconciled. I will stop just *telling* people I'm a Christian and start *showing* them.

Just for today I will quit a bad habit and replace it with one that is good. I will finish a project. I will not minimize or justify my wrong—even my speeding ticket. I will say, "It's my fault," and take the heat for my behavior.

Just for today I will thank God that sometimes "the race is not to the swift or the battle to the strong." For Christ's sake I will delight in my weakness, knowing that "God chose the weak things of the world to shame the strong."

Just for today I will try to live out my faith in very everyday, ordinary ways . . . and trust God in very extraordinary ways. Tomorrow will take care of itself.

See also: Matthew 6:25–34

GOOD COMPANY

If we claim to be without sin, we deceive ourselves and the truth is not in us. If we confess our sins, he is faithful and just and will forgive us our sins and purify us from all unrighteousness.

1 JOHN 1:8–9

From time to time I experiment to see how long I can go without consciously sinning. I don't advertise it like some kind of Guinness contest. It's just a quiet little competition, the results of which are just between me and God.

I remember the time I tried to stop lusting. I wanted to treat girls like people, not as beautiful objects to undress with my eyes. The first day went relatively smoothly. Whenever I saw a girl I felt tempted to ogle, I thanked God for making such an attractive creation. Seriously. I simply whispered a quick, "Boy, God, you sure know your stuff!" I might smile and say hi, but my eyes never lost contact with hers. On the second day, my eyes and will wandered a bit. And I generally blew it the third day by taking second and third glances.

Knowing I can't even last a week without consciously sinning is a spiritual disappointment, because it reminds me how far short of God's standards I fall. Yet I'm not alone. The Bible is full of stories of the "great" men and women of God who fumbled badly themselves. Righteous Noah liked his booze. Abraham sacrificed his wife's chastity for his own safety. Moses frequently blew his stack, and one day sent an Egyptian to the morgue. Rahab ran the best little whorehouse in Jericho. David had a fling with the next-door lady, and then murdered her husband to cover up his sin. Jeremiah drowned his courage in self-pity. John the Baptist doubted Christ's true identity. And that's to say nothing of half the apostles and most of the bit players in the Bible.

It's encouraging to know that I'm in good company: Even those who were most used by God fell short of his holy expectations. They frequently missed his goals by a country mile. I feel a certain kinship with them because they were real people with real weaknesses. Yet God used their lives in mighty ways . . . because they knew they were spiritually bankrupt and sought his forgiveness. And I know God can and *will* do the same for me. His arms are open wide to those who draw near with confession.

As the prophet Isaiah wrote, "Though your sins are like scarlet, they shall be as white as snow; though they are red as crimson, they shall be like wool" (Isaiah 1:18). It's the greatest story ever told.

See also: Isaiah 55:7; Luke 15:11–32

THE MOTORMOUTH

> *In humility consider others better than yourselves.*
> *Each of you should look not only to your own interests, but*
> *also to the interests of others.*
>
> PHILIPPIANS 2:3–4

Janna was home sick one day, and I made the mistake of dropping her assignments by her home after school. She met me at the door with a smile. And from then on she thought of me as a best friend.

A week later she cornered me on the bus ride home after seventh period. She said she just wanted to talk. I kind of shrugged and said, "Sure. I mean, fine." What else could I have said? Then she launched into a rambling, giggling monologue about her sister's new kid, her crazy history teacher, and her appointment to have her wisdom teeth pulled.

"I'll probably be all swelled up like, you know, a pregnant squirrel or something," she said, laughing like she'd told some sort of joke. And all I could think was, *Lord, when is this nut going to shut up and leave?*

Just before stepping off the bus, Janna looked me straight in the eye, flashed a toothy smile and said, "Thanks." I raised my eyebrows and gave her a funny look.

"You know, just for listening. For being, well, a good friend." And then she gave my arm a little grandma pat.

Right out of the blue, just like that.

No kidding, Lord, people never fail to surprise me. Here I do a stupid little thing like drop off her algebra book, and then spend the next few weeks trying to avoid her in the halls and on the bus. This girl—her motormouth bothers me, and I can't understand why she clutches at me almost in desperation, why she thanks me for being a friend. With friends like me, who needs enemies?

Help me, Lord, to understand this odd girl. Help me disregard my pride so I can truly reach out and befriend her . . . like a *real* friend would. And thank you for blinding her to my insensitivity. Just help me to care . . . like you would, Lord.

See also: Romans 12:9–16; Philippians 2:5–8

WINNERS AND LOSERS

You will know that I am the Lord, for you have not followed my decrees or kept my laws but have conformed to the standards of the nations around you.

EZEKIEL 11:12

When you're a kid, you believe in the impossible: reindeer that fly, a fat man that slides down chimneys, rabbits that lay eggs. You also believe you'll grow up to be a winner, like maybe a tennis champ or TV reporter. Perhaps even the President.

But when you actually *do* grow up, you realize you've been duped. All that talk about Rudolph and Santa and the Easter Bunny was fairy tale. And the hope you had of being a winner began to seem equally absurd. Along with high school you discover you'll never be as successful as those around you. You flunk a French test. You get chosen last in P.E. You sit home Friday nights. Meanwhile, everyone else seems to be getting the awards, the lead roles, the friends, the scholarships, the dates, the attention.

You feel like a loser, but don't want to let on. You just try all the harder to be a winner. Maybe you'll be OK if you keep trying to fit in, gain acceptance somehow, and stop the familiar fog of depression and frustration from creeping behind your eyes.

It's easy, you think. Maybe things will come together . . . if you just try a new fad diet . . . if you just get some decent clothes . . . if you just use cologne . . . if you just listen to different music . . . if you just act a little more together and try some new things.

Pretty soon you've got yourself convinced: What harm can really come if I experiment a little and "go all the way" or smoke a couple of funny cigarettes or get smashed once or twice? I mean, what harm can it *really* do?

214

Before long, you're listening not to the "still small voice of God," but to Hollywood celebrities and hot-talking DJs and rock 'n' roll raunchies and semiliterate athletes who rake in $3 million a year. And by their standards, if you dare call them that, we all fall short. Success will always be one rung higher.

Because we are Christians, our success ought to be gauged by our changed lives. Period. But no lives will ever change if we're living by the world's standards and trying to win at all costs.

It's not that God has such a huge grudge against winning. It's just that most of us spend too much time trying to win the wrong contests.

See also: Romans 12:2; 1 Corinthians 1:18–31

LEARNING TO TRUST

Trust in the Lord with all your heart and lean not on your own understanding; in all your ways acknowledge him, and he will make your paths straight.

PROVERBS 3:5–6

When I was a kid learning to swim, I gripped the pool's edge until my knuckles turned white. But my instructor thought I could learn faster if I let go. Since she was also my mother, I thought I could trust her. So I took a deep breath, loosened my fingers . . . and just about drowned. I thrashed the water into a whirlpool trying to stay afloat. And the harder I kicked and splashed, the quicker I sank.

"Don't fight the water," my mother said, slipping her hand beneath my back. "Trust it to hold you up, and use your strength to propel you." She slowly removed her hand, leaving me buoyed flat on my back. "I'm floating, I'm actually floating!" I said with a huge smile. Over the next few months, I learned I could not only trust the water to support me, but also swim the distance of the pool.

I find that learning to trust God is like learning to swim. The hardest part is simply letting go and trusting God for such things as finding a job, coping with the death of a close friend or relative, working out hassles at home or school, dealing with the pressures of temptation. You may agonize over your uncertainties and insecurities. But God is there to support those who trust in his certainty and security. To you he promises a future and a hope.

As Isaiah writes, "Those who hope in the Lord will renew their strength. They will soar on wings like eagles; they will run and not grow weary, they will walk and not be faint."

The verbs he uses are all action words. The action begins when you make your first move.

See also: Psalm 37:3–4; 139:1–2; Jeremiah 29:11

ON THE ROAD

In all your ways acknowledge him, and he will make your paths straight.

PROVERBS 3:6

From the observation deck atop Chicago's 100-story John Hancock Building, bits of clouds rush by within arm's reach, and sailboats dot Lake Michigan some 1,000 feet below like kids' toys in a backyard pool. Eight lanes of traffic snake along Lake Shore Drive. They carve a path between million-dollar condos and the waterfront, fueling a spaghetti-like network of expressways that lead to the outskirts of Chicago and suburbs beyond.

Sharing the observation deck with sightseers is a traffic control center, manned by a radio technician who uses a powerful telescope to monitor the maze of autos during rush peaks. But he doesn't just watch—he broadcasts things like: "There's a twenty-five-minute delay on the inbound Eisenhower Expressway due to a jack-knifed semi. Detour at Ogden." He points out the stalled cars, the accidents, the construction delays—the paths that should generally be avoided—and guides drivers along the route he feels is best, according to his broader perspective.

Not all drivers tune in to his station. Those who don't must necessarily choose their own route, based on a ground-level perspective. They may dodge and dart from lane to lane, thinking they are gaining time. But for all they know, the highway may be blocked just up ahead. The problem: they can't see much beyond their own front bumper.

In our day-to-day lives, we're much like these misguided drivers. We rely on our own limited perspective as we face our futures and the road up ahead. "There is a way that *seems* right to a man," the Bible says, "but in the end it leads to death." *The road is blocked,* but you can know that only if you're in tune with God, who views the world like a traffic controller scoping the roadways that stretch from horizon to horizon. He sees the roads you roam—where you've been and where you're headed. He knows where the detours are.

But God doesn't just watch—he *directs.* You're not just another somebody lost in the honky-honk rush of life. You're a unique creation of his that he will lovingly guide along the route he feels is best for you, according to his broader perspective.

Tune in today. Allow the one who is above all to "make your paths straight."

See also: Proverbs 14:12; Isaiah 42:16; 46:10

THE FIRST MOVE

Love your neighbor as yourself.

LUKE 10:27

When the divorce papers were filed, Randy's father loaded his belongings into a U-Haul and pulled out of Randy's life in a cloud of dust. He settled in a small house nearby, but he might as well have moved to another continent, because he never called or stopped by.

At night Randy often did his homework by the phone, hoping his father might decide to call. But as days blurred into weeks without word from his dad, Randy sensed it was a case of out of sight, out of mind.

Then one day Randy decided he wouldn't wait for his father to make the first move. He might not see him again if he did. So he screwed up his courage and stopped by his dad's new house.

"How long's it been?" he asked Randy when his son entered.

"Three months."

"No kidding. Has it really been that long?" His father muttered something about being so busy, then showed him his place: lawn chairs as living room furniture; TV on a crate; cheap foam pads thrown down as a mattress, no dresser.

"It's not much, but it's livable," his father said.

Randy nodded and forced a smile. It hurt to see his father living like that. And in that moment, he saw his dad not as his own father, but as a person in desperate need. He probably hadn't called because he felt no one really cared about him. Maybe he thought everyone blamed him for the divorce.

Suddenly Randy turned to his dad and hugged him tightly. And in the middle of the embrace, he silently asked God to help him love his father with the love of the Lord.

In the Bible, Christ says we are to love our neighbor as ourselves. It's presented not as a suggestion, but as a command. And it's no less of a command when your "neighbor" happens to be your own father.

See also: Colossians 3:12–14; 1 John 3:16–18; 4:19–21

WEEK

19

A WORD OF THANKS

Enter his gates with thanksgiving and his courts with praise; give thanks to him and praise his name. For the Lord is good and his love endures forever; his faithfulness continues through all generations.

PSALM 100:4–5

I could talk about problems. There are plenty of those. But today, Lord, I want to say thanks ... for friends and freckles and footrests and Frisbees; for footballs, fireflies, flamingos, and fathers. For cartoons and Christmas and cash (when I've got it); for campfires, cashews, Coke and ... ahem, commodes, I thank you this day.

My creator, I thank you for graham crackers, grandparents, graduation, good grades. Not to forget hamburgers, heartthrobs, home and homecoming, the four-minute mile, and coaches that smile.

Ever-loving God, I offer thanks for Jell-O, jukeboxes, June, and July, for jeans that fade and dreams that don't. In addition, for small mistakes and big erasers, for music that's good, librarians that laugh, chairs that swivel, and hiccups that stop, I voice my praise.

God of glory, I'm grateful for breath mints and beaches, popcorn and pizza, dreams and drive-throughs, weekends and winks, as well as a mother's hugs, stingerless bugs and chocolate taste ... without the chocolate waist. And my sincerest thanks for "You've never looked better!" "Welcome home!" "The exam's been canceled!" "Take a day off!" and "Keep the change!"

And most of all, dear Father, I thank you for yourself: the King of all kings, author of love, giver of life beyond life and hope in despair.

For these things and easily a hundred thousand others, I offer this prayer.

See also: Ephesians 5:19–20; Philippians 4:4,8

FOLLOW THE LEADER

The Lord himself goes before you and will be with you; he will never leave you nor forsake you. Do not be afraid; do not be discouraged.

DEUTERONOMY 31:8

Our school football coach was like a member of the CIA—a super sleuth of sorts, who often sneaked into pregame practices of the opposing team.

Sitting in the stands undetected, he'd scout their biggest and best players, analyze their plays, determine their weaknesses, and log notes about the condition of the playing field. If there was a gouge in the turf on the 40-yard line or a puddle in the corner of the end zone, he knew about it. And based on all of this foreknowledge, he'd compile a game plan—a strategy of attack that he then communicated to our team.

Come game time, his advance work paid off. Every play was engineered to pit our strengths against the opponent's weaknesses. Naturally, he could not play the game for us—*we* had to carry the ball. But we carried it best when we followed his instructions. And we could always count on him to stand behind the team, directing, rooting, encouraging, challenging.

The same is true of your relationship with God. You don't know what kinds of challenges you'll face next week, next month, next year. You don't know where your future will lead. But God does, because he's scouted ahead.

"The Lord himself goes before you," the Bible says. God has seen what lies up the road. He has scouted the opposition, and he knows every obstacle, every rut and puddle that stands between you and ultimate victory.

But God doesn't just go before you and then recline in the stands, quiet and smug, as you blunder along. He goes the next step and "will be with you." Yes, God knows all about who you'll marry, where you'll go to school, where you'll work. He knows in detail the struggles you'll face. And he's right at your side, directing, rooting, encouraging, and challenging.

The Bible offers the ultimate assurance that God "will never leave you nor forsake you." *Never.* He's with you from now through eternity. You needn't be afraid, nor discouraged. You need only follow the Leader.

See also: Isaiah 42:16; 49:10

ON YOUR MARK ...

> *Since we are surrounded by such a great cloud of witnesses, let us throw off everything that hinders and the sin that so easily entangles, and let us run with perseverance the race marked out for us.*

Hᴇʙʀᴇᴡꜱ 12:1

Sports analogies are frequently used in the Bible to describe hard-to-understand spiritual concepts. Swimming, wrestling, and boxing are among the sports mentioned. In the passage above, the writer of Hebrews uses running to explain "faithfulness." Maintaining a long-term relationship with God, he says, is like preparing for a difficult race: say, for example, the Boston Marathon.

Lacing up your first pair of Nikes can be deceiving. You feel like you can outrun Flo Jo or sprint faster than Carl Lewis. It's just your imagination.

After jogging a few blocks, you wheeze like an old smoker with emphysema. Stripping off your sweats helps. But after struggling another couple of blocks, you duck behind a tree and glance around quickly. Then you barf the Three Musketeers and Doritos you had for breakfast, wipe your mouth, and head for home.

Only after months of long, hard workouts do things come easier. Your endurance and speed pick up. You drop some weight. Your muscles are toned. After a year or so, you think more seriously about Boston. It seems like an attainable goal.

But . . . you can't help noticing that when you run, you run alone. Your friends, who used to invite you out on Friday nights, no longer bother. Some think you're crazy. It crosses your mind that maybe they're right. Perhaps you *are* overdoing it.

So you take some time off. You revert to junk food and late-night parties. You sleep in. But fitness, unlike body fat, cannot be stored, and soon you're out of shape again. The entry deadline for the race passes unnoticed. And you end up watching ESPN reports about the marathon from your dad's easy chair.

The author of Hebrews wasn't a letterman in track. But he knew enough about marathons and enough about being a Christian to know neither is a cakewalk. Both require all-out effort. You can't worry about others, or you'll lose your focus. Persistence and endurance are musts. Certain things you must do without. Attitude is essential.

And then after all the training and preparation, you've got to hit the track and run like the wind if you want to receive the prize. No race—not even a figurative one—can be won by sitting on your laurels. You just can't get far in an easy chair.

See also: 1 Corinthians 9:24–27; Hebrews 10:36–39

KING OF HEARTS

After the people saw the miraculous sign that Jesus did, they began to say, "Surely this is the Prophet who is to come into the world." Jesus, knowing that they

*intended to come and make him king by force, withdrew
again into the hills by himself.*

JOHN 6:14–16

Jesus could have had a cushy job in politics for the asking.
He had the charisma and magnetism campaign managers drool
about. Barely 30, his political future seemed bright. But he had a
hard time convincing people he didn't want his name on the ballot.

Take, for example, the day he retreated with his apostles to
a remote shore of the Sea of Galilee. It was a favorite spot where they
could be alone to pray, swim, fish, or just lay out and get some sun.
However, a crowd of thousands tracked him to their hideaway. Some
simply wanted to shake his hand and perhaps get an autograph. But
most came because they were sick and tired of being sick and tired.

One look at the diseased multitudes, and the apostles voted
to send them away. Half were probably contagious. But Jesus rolled
up his sleeves and spent the rest of his day healing everyone he
could get his hands on. And then toward nightfall he took a few
loaves and fishes and whipped together a picnic feast that more than
fed everyone—even those wanting seconds and thirds.

After supper, the crowd got a bit rowdy. The fast-food miracle convinced many that Jesus was the Messiah who was to come and
rule his people. They believed his kingdom would be a strong-arm
political force that would drive out their enemies and provide peace
and independence. You can almost hear the people starting to chant:
"JEE-ZUSSS! JEE-ZUSSS!" You can almost see the campaign buttons: *Jesus, King of the Jews.* But their candidate didn't hang around
for speeches. He pulled up his toga and hightailed it for the hills.

Christ didn't usually run from confrontation, even when
people conspired against him. But now they conspired *for* him. He
insisted his kingdom was not of the earthly sort—of marble halls and
golden thrones. Nevertheless, "King of the Jews" was a tag that stuck
with him until death.

Christ probably would have preferred something more along the line of "King of Hearts," a tag that has stuck now some 2,000 years.

See also: Luke 17:20–21; Revelation 3:20

REVERSED AMERICAN STANDARDS

> *Blessed are the poor in spirit, ... those who mourn, ... the meek, ... those who hunger and thirst for righteousness, ... the merciful, ... the pure in heart, ... the peacemakers, ... those who are persecuted because of righteousness, for theirs is the kingdom of heaven.*
>
> MATTHEW 5:3–10

When the final class was finished and the locker halls quiet ... when the stereos had been clicked off and the glossy magazines closed ... when the sun had set and day was done ... the people snuggled under covers with these thoughts numbing their minds to sleep:

Blessed are the wealthy, for theirs is the kingdom on earth. They will have no needs and will charge the desires of their hearts at Nordstroms and Saks.

Blessed are the merrymakers, for they will get invited to the best parties and never be lonely or sit by themselves at lunch.

Blessed are the arrogant, for they can stomp without being stomped in return. Their way through life will be paved by the weak and the meek.

Blessed are those who change with the times, for they will never be caught by surprise. They will know what's in and what's out, who's hot and who's not. They'll never wear the wrong label or tell old jokes.

Blessed are the steel-hearted, for they are masters of their emotions. Their mascara will never run.

Blessed are those whose morals are flexible, for they will never feel awkward. Nor will they be haunted by a nagging conscience.

Blessed are the troublemakers, for they will never wait in line.

Blessed are those who are chastised for their craftiness and unyielding ambition, for they will rise above their critics.

Blessed are you when people pat you on the back, praise you, and admit you into their inner circle. Rejoice and be glad, because great is your reward on earth, for in the same way they honored the winners who came before you.

Yes, blessed are you winners, for you will always feel secure in yourself. And when you snuggle under the covers, close your eyes, and drift deep into sleep, don't be surprised if your hellish nightmare is not a nightmare at all.

See also: Proverbs 16:18; Luke 12:15–21; 1 Corinthians 10:12

THE LIST MAKER

Man is destined to die once, and after that to face judgment.

HEBREWS 9:27

Bonnie was the most organized person I ever knew. Her life was regulated by a daily schedule, which included everything from *shower–6:20 a.m.* to *remove makeup–8:40 p.m.* She was always referring to one list or another: *Things to Do-Wah-Diddy Today, Things to Remember, Things to Buy,* and *People to Call.* She planned for everything, and was never surprised.

We were talking once when the subject of God came up. A relative had died, and I happened to mention how glad I was this person was a Christian. Bonnie looked at me funny. "God's a cop-out," she finally said. "People have to face reality and take charge of their own lives." And then she pulled a small binder out of her purse and showed me her *Goals List*, which was divided into weekly goals, monthly goals, and future goals. On the list was everything from the books she would read in the coming months, offices she would run for in student-body elections, the type of guy she would eventually marry, etc. She placed a red check mark next to goals she had already attained.

Well, Bonnie was so disciplined that she met every one of her goals in years to come. She earned her varsity letter in volleyball and read *War and Peace* her junior year; was elected class president her senior year; attended a prestigious university; worked for a big newspaper back East; married a doctor; drove an antique Triumph; and lived in a two-story colonial—just as she had planned.

Everything was perfect ... until she had a fatal traffic accident and woke up in hell. It was the one thing she hadn't planned on.

See also: Luke 16:19–31; Romans 6:23

POINTS TO PONDER–HELL

When the Son of Man comes in his glory, and all the angels with him, he will sit on his throne in heavenly glory. All the nations will be gathered before him, and he will separate the people one from another as a shepherd separates the sheep from the goats. He will put the sheep on his right and the goats on his left. Then the King will say to those on his right, "Come, you who are blessed by my Father; take your inheritance, the kingdom prepared for you since the creation of the world." Then he will say to those on his left, "Depart from me, you who are cursed, into the eternal fire prepared for the devil and his angels."

MATTHEW 25:31–34, 41

The road to hell is paved with good intentions.

KARL MARX

Hell was not prepared for man. God never meant that man would ever go to hell. Hell was prepared for the devil and his angels, but man rebelled against God and followed the devil. Hell is essentially and basically banishment from the presence of God for deliberately rejecting Jesus Christ as Lord and Savior.

BILLY GRAHAM

The one principle of hell is "I am on my own."

GEORGE MacDONALD

All hope abandon, ye who enter here.

DANTE (INSCRIPTION OVER GATEWAY TO HELL)

The road to hell is thick with taxicabs.

DON HEROLD

To be in hell is to drift; to be in heaven is to steer.

GEORGE BERNARD SHAW

In all discussions of hell we should keep steadily before our eyes the possible damnation, not of our enemies nor our friends . . . but of ourselves.

C. S. LEWIS

Fear not that your life shall come to an end, but rather that it shall never have a beginning.

JOHN HENRY NEWMAN

The choices of time are binding in eternity.

JACK MacARTHUR

I willingly believe that the damned are, in one sense, successful, rebels to the end; that the doors of hell are locked on the *inside*. I do not mean that the ghosts may not *wish* to come out of hell, in the vague fashion wherein an envious man "wishes" to be happy: but ... they enjoy forever the horrible freedom they have demanded, and are therefore self-enslaved just as the blessed, forever submitting to obedience, become through all eternity more and more free.

C. S. LEWIS

The mission of Jesus cannot be defined without speaking of man being lost.

HENRI BLOCHER

The wicked work harder to reach hell than the righteous to reach heaven.

JOSH BILLINGS

See also: Isaiah 14:12–15; Luke 12:5

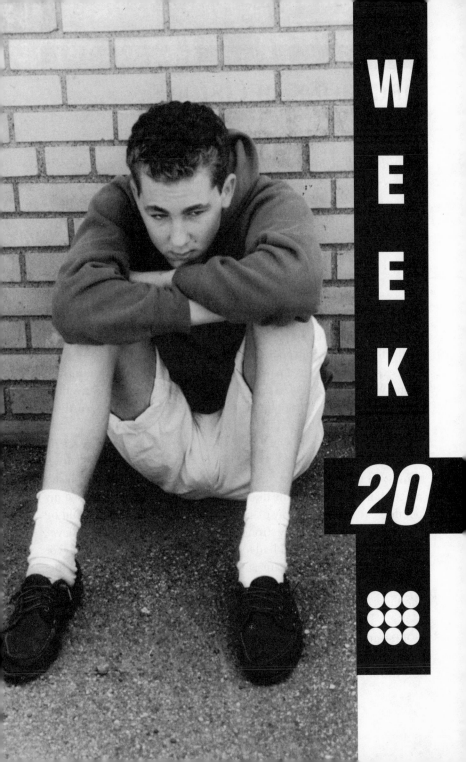

WEEK

20

DECISIONS, DECISIONS, DECISIONS

If anyone comes to me and does not hate his father and mother, his wife and children, his brothers and sisters—yes, even his own life—he cannot be my disciple.

LUKE 14:26

Making decisions has never come easy to me. I'm at my worst in a restaurant. The waiter will come to the table with his pencil and pad, and I'll say something like, "How is the chili tonight?"

As he begins to tell me, another item catches my eye. "I think, maybe, I'll order a BLT instead, with fries ... except I always have that. What's the Chef's Special?"

When I contemplated faith in Christ, the decision was especially difficult. My conversion wasn't a euphoric fireworks-and-tears type experience. It was a painful, anguishing process of counting the costs: What would it mean to my goals and ambitions? How would it affect my family and friends? Was being a Christian really worth it? It was the biggest choice I'd ever make.

I knew that by saying yes to God I had to *comparatively* say no to everything else; by loving God I had to *comparatively* hate all other things. In using the word "hate" in the verse above, Christ doesn't mean that I treat my family like Nazi henchmen who have gassed my pet dog. It's simply his way of saying that my love for him should be infinitely deeper, infinitely stronger than any other love I might have.

Because of that, I had to *comparatively* relinquish my devotion to my desires and dreams, to my family, and even to my own life. I knew God demanded my complete devotion. Not a part—not even the biggest part. All of it.

That's what Moses meant when he told the Israelites: "The LORD our God, the LORD is one. Love the LORD your God with all your heart and with all your soul and with all your strength." If they loved God as directed—with their full emotional, mental, and physical capabilities—that didn't leave room for them to *really* love anything else. But then, God has no peers, no partners. If he's truly Lord, his throne cannot be shared.

I once saw a bumper sticker that read, "Things go better with Christ." It was a takeoff on the old Coca-Cola commercials. But God never intended things to "Go better with Christ," as though he were the Coke that perfectly complements a burger and fries. No, he is the meal. And when we choose him, we must necessarily forsake all other loves.

It's certainly not an easy choice. But it is a choice God demands we make.

See also: Deuteronomy 6:4, 5, 13; Mark 8:34–38

ONE OF THE GANG

Let us purify ourselves from everything that contaminates body and spirit, perfecting holiness out of reverence for God.

2 CORINTHIANS 7:1

When it comes right down to it, most people are probably uncomfortable with the word "holy." It makes you think of nuns and angels and retired ministers. It's definitely not the label I wanted to be known by. In my school yearbooks, my friends used a lot of different words to describe me. They scribbled little notes, saying I was ... oh, "a great friend" ... "fun-loving" ... "a great guy to hang around with" ... "funny, in a different kind of way"—things like that.

No one said I was "holy." Holiness just wasn't the goal I aspired to.

Maybe that's because my first concern was seldom God—it was *myself.* My self-worth was often defined by how well I was accepted by others. I wanted to fit in. Sure, I was a Christian, I just didn't want to be *too* Christian. As a result, I often compromised my innermost beliefs about what I knew was right and wrong. With a crowd of Christians I could act very Christian. But change my surroundings and I'd turn color like a chameleon to blend right in. I'd do whatever it took to be "one of the gang."

After times like that, God always seemed distant. Maybe it was because I hadn't "acted like a Christian should." I knew God wasn't fooled with an act or outward appearance. He searched my heart—and we both knew I had compromised myself. To gain the respect of others, I had lost respect for myself. And the greater need behind self-respect is the inner assurance of feeling accepted by God.

By God's standards for our lives, we all fall short. We conform to the pattern of the world when the Bible warns against it. We mimic the lives of unbelievers when we should mirror Christ. In effect, we've turned holiness into a bad word.

"Be holy, because I am holy," the Lord said.

On your own that's as impossible to attain as growing another foot in height. But we're assured in Philippians 2:13 that we're not struggling alone. God is at work in us to *help* us desire and attain his standard and purpose for our lives. It's just a matter of allowing him enough elbow room to do the job.

See also: Romans 12:2; 2 Corinthians 6:14; 1 Thessalonians 4:3–8; 1 Peter 1:13–16

NO ORDINARY PEOPLE

> *The LORD said to [Moses], "What is that in your hand?" "A staff," he replied. The LORD said, "Throw it on the ground."*
>
> EXODUS 4:2–3

When you become a Christian, the thought of being used by God to "make a difference" in people's lives can paralyze you with insecurity. Your brain is gripped by the thought that you have such plain talents. You feel so ordinary, so insignificant. But God's outlook is different. With him there are no ordinary people.

When I wrestle with insecurity, I like to review the first chapters of Exodus where God tells an "ordinary" jelly-willed shepherd named Moses that he'll be used by God to confront the Egyptians, the most powerful nation on earth. But the withering, self-doubting Moses promptly stutters several reasons why he *can't* do what God says he *can* do.

Finally, God directs his attention to the plainest prop in the vicinity: the dead, dirty staff of wood Moses carried. When he obeys God's command to throw it on the ground, the walking stick becomes a slithering, hissing snake. When Moses picks it up again, it reverts to wood.

A celestial magic show? No, just God demonstrating that he can use what is ordinary to us in extraordinary ways. The key is Exodus 4:20: The staff of Moses had become the "staff of God."

More importantly, Moses had become the "Moses of God." He finally realized that what he felt *incapable* to do, God was *able* to do. And in the succeeding chapters of Exodus, you'll read the story of how God used this "ordinary" shepherd and "ordinary" rod to perform numerous miracles and alter the course of human history.

The same thing happened with the twelve disciples chosen by Christ to convey his message to the world. They were a ragtag group Christ selected from wharves and back alleys, not from marble palaces or judicial chambers. But they were willing to follow the Lord—to become "men of God."

In a sense, God's in the business of making "somebodies" out of "nobodies." And in his eyes, there are no ordinary people— just people either willing or unwilling to follow him. This is the challenge we must each face individually: Am I *really* the "Andrea of God," the "Scott of God," the "_____ of God" that the Lord wants me to be? Nobody can answer that but *you.*

See also: Proverbs 3:5–6; Luke 9:23–26

OPINION POLL

"Who do you say I am?" Simon Peter answered,
"You are the Christ, the Son of the living God."

MATTHEW 16:15–16

George Gallup has made millions by asking people questions. His biggest business comes during election years when would-be congressmen, senators, and presidents seek his help conducting random surveys to determine where they stand in the public eye. Is anything they say getting through? They want to know.

Jesus had a similar concern during the three years he spent traveling about the Palestine countryside some 2,000 years ago. Wherever he went, he attracted massive crowds of people. They sometimes followed him night and day, even when they had no food. Never before had someone performed the kinds of miracles he did: healing the sick, raising the dead, calming the storm-tossed seas, multiplying a sack lunch into a lavish picnic for thousands. And never before had anyone made the kinds of claims he did: to be the one and only Son of God, the bread of life, the forgiver of sin, the only way by which people might know God the Father.

But did the public believe him? Was anything he said getting through? Christ wanted to know.

He didn't have the benefit of a sophisticated polling service. Taking a random survey was unheard of. So he relied heavily on his disciples for feedback. One day he asked them, "Who do people say the Son of Man is?" Their reply: "Some say John the Baptist; others say Elijah; and still others, Jeremiah or one of the prophets."

This public confusion probably stung Christ. People knew *about* him, but they didn't know him as he wanted to be known. He was fixed in the public's eye. But he was not yet firmly implanted in their hearts as Lord.

Suddenly Christ fired another question: "But what about you? Who do you say I am?" he asked the twelve, his closest companions.

"You are the Christ," Simon Peter said firmly, "the Son of the living God."

Peter hit the proverbial nail smack dab on the head. Jesus' message was *finally* getting through. And if Jesus ever felt like dashing into Peter's arms and giving him a rib-crushing hug, I'm sure he did at that moment.

See also: Matthew 10:32; Acts 2:36

MATTERS OF CONSCIENCE

I strive always to keep my conscience clear before God and man.

ACTS 24:16

I had some time to kill before my next class, so I stopped by the library. Flipping through a dog-eared magazine, I discovered a humorous story about the government's "Conscience Fund."

Guilt has a way of nagging at some people—people such as the man who sent a buck to Washington to pay for the bottle of typewriter oil he stole while serving in the Air Force years before ... or the former federal employee who mailed $157 to the fund to make up for the nights he had left work early ... or the New Yorker who bought an air-mail stamp to return a penny he said belonged to the government.

I chuckled through most of the story. But then I began to wonder *why* I was laughing. After all, what was *really* so funny about people who simply wanted to be able to look at themselves in the mirror while brushing their teeth? Was it humorous that their code of ethics was stronger than my own as a Christian?

The "small wrongs" they couldn't live with were not that different from the ones I regularly ignored or rationalized. That struck me—just as I was about to rip the story out of the magazine for future reference. *Who's going to miss an article they wouldn't read anyway?* I excused myself.

It was reinforced the next day when I wrote a letter to a friend but didn't have any postage. So I began peeling an uncanceled stamp from another letter to use again. *No big deal—it's just a stamp,* I thought.

Later that day I was nearly to the post office when I noticed I was driving 10 mph over the speed limit. *But everyone is going that fast,* I rationalized.

And I kept the extra dime the postal clerk mistakenly gave me. *It's just small change,* I reasoned.

These were all little wrongs—things that really didn't hurt anyone else. Still, I was amazed how often and easily I minimized them. I had been living as if only the "big" stuff—the *real grossies*—mattered, and had developed a callousness toward small infractions. I had fooled myself into thinking that living as a Christian involved more than just following Christ's righteous pattern of life in very ordinary, everyday ways.

I can't say my life has changed drastically since that realization hit. And yet I find myself being a little more literal about right and wrong. I weigh my small decisions more carefully, knowing that will help me with big decisions.

Each day has become an experiment in which I, like Paul, strive to keep my conscience clear before God and man. It can be a very radical way of living.

See also: 1 Peter 1:15–16

EVERYONE LIKES BABIES

The time came for the baby to be born, and she gave birth to her firstborn, a son. She wrapped him in strips of cloth and placed him in a manger, because there was no room for them in the inn.

LUKE 2:6–7

Everyone likes babies. There is something inherently cute about them, regardless of looks—something that brings out the child in normally mature, reserved adults. Just watch their reactions outside any hospital nursery.

I suppose people thought Jesus was kind of cute, too, as he lay in the feed trough with bits of rolled oats and hay clinging to his bunting. If you could just get over the smell of cow dung that hung in the air, you could watch for hours as he drooled and bubbled and cooed. But baby Jesus grew up fast—and as he did, people's reactions changed dramatically.

As a man, Christ presented the sternest challenge ever made to mankind. He was vocal—some thought belligerent—about his beliefs, and a contract was put out on his life to shut him up. Everywhere he went he was trailed by a hit squad. People got riled when he claimed he was visiting earth on a special mission from God. All of a sudden, it was not good enough to be a mind-your-own-business Jew, to go to synagogue, clean up after your dog, and not spit in the marketplace. Christ changed the rules of the game overnight by saying he was the way to God—the only way—and that no one could come to God except through him. It was the worst news some people had received in years.

More than that, Jesus demanded people's total allegiance, and frequently reminded them that such loyalty would separate entire families and set father against son, mother against daughter. He never promised that his followers would win friends and influence people. He said they would be scorned.

Had Christ been a little more moderate in his statements, he would have been left alone. But he stuck to his guns and the Jewish mafia finally caught up with him. In the centuries that have come and gone since, it's odd how many people forget how truly radical Christ

239

was. At Christmas, churches fill to capacity with people who come to hear the story of a baby born to two hick Jews in a stinky barn.

Everyone likes babies—especially baby saviors. They forget, however, that the baby grew up.

See also: Matthew 10:34–39; Luke 14:28–33; 16:13

TWO OLD GEEZERS

I give you this charge: Preach the Word; be pre-pared in season and out of season.

2 TIMOTHY 4:1–2

If anyone needed to know the Lord, I figured it was old man Chambers and his wife, Gladys. They lived two doors down, and when I'd leave for church on Sunday mornings, I'd see them sitting in lawn-chair rockers beneath the shade of their dying elm tree. He'd be reading a copy of some movie magazine; she'd be chain-smoking Winstons and watching jays through a pair of opera glasses.

Mr. Chambers had worked highway construction, and I used to marvel at his strength when I was a kid. "Go ahead, feel the mus-cle," he'd say, and would then pump his biceps till it seemed his arm would pop. But his arms had grown thin and veiny over the inter-vening fifteen years, and his once-smooth voice grated like a cement truck in low gear. The neighborhood gossip now was that they both had liver and lung problems—too much booze and too much smoking.

I found it easy to wave as I drove by their house. It was the polite thing to do—you know, "Be nice to old people." But I could never get up the courage to actually stop the car, get out, and talk with them. After I became a Christian, I often thought of how God could fill their lives with purpose. They always looked so lonely sit-ting out front, but I was busy and, well, there were things to do, places to go, people to see. Besides, what would I say? "Hi, sure is nice to talk with you after fifteen years. Great weather, uh, by the way, do you know Jesus loves you?"

As months passed, I convinced myself I was just on a guilt trip, feeling overly weird about two old people who really didn't matter to me. And then one winter night as I was getting ready for bed, I heard the wail of fire engines nearby. I grabbed my jacket and darted out the door. Flames were shooting from the Chamberses' house, and a crowd was gathering.

I thought, great, the Lord will show me some way to befriend them after the fire. All the waving I'd done would finally pay off. Then I saw the firemen drag two bodies from the house and cover them with blankets until the county coroner could arrive.

I will never forget that scene. To this day it's tattooed on my brain. I see the snow, feel the cold, smell the smoke. And then there are the bodies—a vivid reminder that doors of opportunity God opens for us don't stay open forever.

See also: Isaiah 52:7; Matthew 28:18–20; 2 Timothy 4:2

WEEK

21

TEAM SPIRIT

Let us not give up meeting together, as some are in the habit of doing, but let us encourage one another – and all the more as you see the Day approaching.

HEBREWS 10:25

Why bother with church? Why can't I just worship God alone on the bank of a river, in a pine forest, or better yet, in bed with the covers pulled tight around my shoulders? I can meditate about the Lord as easily in the hammock out back as in a hard pew. I can sing hymns in the shower as well as I can in a sanctuary.

Today, and for the rest of the week, we'll address these concerns and try to dredge up some answers to the question: Do I really need church? Why?

I need church because I'm a member of the team.

Imagine my excitement if, after weeks of grueling tryouts, I wandered by the gym after school and saw my name posted on the final football team roster. Just as I'm about ready to whoop it up, the head coach rounds the corner and slaps me on the back, saying, "Way to go, Bruiser! You made the cut. I'll see you at the first team meeting – Tuesday at six."

But what if my response was, "Hey, Coach, terrific! I can't tell you how much it means to make the team. But one question: What's this about a team meeting? They're kind of a drag, if you know what I mean. Besides, Tuesday nights are sort of bad for me – my favorite TV show is on. How about letting me know if anything important happens. Or, tell you what, how about just stopping by the house afterward? I'll put on some popcorn, and you can relay the highlights of what you told the team ..."

This scenario is understandably absurd. By skipping the team meeting, I'd miss a big part of what it means to be a team member. Team meetings are called to renew spirits and gather perspective – perhaps after a loss the week before. It's a time to organize strategy for next week; a time of retreat that provides a temporary sanctuary from the clamoring crowds. It's a time of encouragement when the coach challenges the team and offers advice. And being together generates team spirit—a spirit that can't be duplicated on my own.

As head of the church, Jesus Christ has called us to meet together. We're members of his team, and there are some things he'd like to tell us.

See also: Matthew 18:20; Colossians 4:7–9

FAMILY MATTERS

Just as each of us has one body with many members, and these members do not all have the same function, so in Christ we who are many form one body, and each member belongs to all the others.

ROMANS 12:4–5

Why bother with church? Attending services on Sunday doesn't make me a Christian any more than climbing a tree makes me a monkey. If my relationship with God began as a personal matter, then why gather with old men in sport coats, gray-haired grandmothers, screaming kids, and hypocrites?

Do I really need church? Why?

I need church because it is a family reunion.

A family reunion is composed not only of people my age, but also of old folks who snooze in the shade, nursing mothers and their whining infants, neat-as-a-pin aunts, raucous uncles, slobber-mouthed cousins, parents, and yapping dogs.

Before the weekend reunion is over, Junior will break a window with his Frisbee, Aunt Becki and Uncle Dave will not be speaking to each other, Grandma will finish knitting another afghan, I will be told fifteen times that I have my great-grandfather's eyes,

Grandpa will lose his glasses, Uncle Scott will tell the same, dumb joke six times, my brother will get sick behind a tree from too much lime-Jell-O-and-carrot salad, the dog will tree the cat, and most people will be sniffling. Really, there's nothing quite like it.

Reunions are important because they bring together a diversity of people who have not led perfect lives, married saints, and raised kids that don't mash peas on the wall. Each person, myself included, is imperfect—but we remain linked to each other by reason of a common heritage.

Together, we're a melting pot of people who have overlooked our differences to thrive as a family through sickness and health, births and deaths, successes and failures. By holding reunions, we affirm the importance of family and create a sense of unity that spans generations.

As head of the church, Jesus Christ has slated regular family reunions. Every week. As his children, we are privileged to share in these ongoing gatherings that affirm family ties and bridge both years and idiosyncrasies.

See also: Romans 12:6–8; 1 Corinthians 12:12–31

TIME OUT

By the seventh day God had finished the work he had been doing; so on the seventh day he rested from all his work. And God blessed the seventh day and made it holy, because on it he rested from all the work of creating that he had done.

GENESIS 2:2–3

Why bother with church? My life is so hectic already that attending Sunday services is just another item on my pressure-cooker list of things to do. I've got three chapters to read for history, a five-page paper due in English, my dad is on me to clean the garage, the oil in my car needs to be changed, and my friends think I am ignoring them. I don't think my schedule can take any additional strain at this point.

Do I really need church? Why?

I need church because it is a retreat.

When I get so busy that I have no time for church, then I'm simply too busy. It may be just another item on my "Things to Do" list, but it's one of the most important because it gives me time to stop, gather my perspective, reflect on the coming week, and to "be still" and meditate with God.

It's a time to ungarble my mind, restring my nerves, and calm my churning stomach. Church is a place to realign priorities, to worship God, and celebrate Christ's empty tomb. *Celebrate*—yes, that's the word. By no means should church be Dullsville.

In the first chapter of Genesis, the Bible details how, in six days, God created everything from cotton-candy clouds, snails, and monster surf at Sunset Beach ... to the whiskered walrus, Venus fly trap, and lightning bolts. And on the seventh day he took a breather: "God blessed the seventh day and made it holy, because on it he rested from all the work of creating that he had done."

Jesus often did the same by retreating with his disciples to a sanctuary, a hiding place, where they could release their heavy loads of anxiety, strengthen their slender threads of patience and, most of all, *remember* their heavenly Father.

As head of the church, Jesus Christ has called for us to take weekly breathers—to rest up, to celebrate ... and to remember.

See also: Psalm 46:10; Matthew 11:28; John 14:27; 1 Corinthians 11:23–26

HOSPITAL TREATMENT

It is not the healthy who need a doctor, but the sick.
I have not come to call the righteous, but sinners.

MARK 2:17

Why bother with church? I can understand why some Christians go every Sunday—they're basically loser types. But I've got talent and confidence. So why can't I just skip the stained-glass, hard pews, pipe organ, and preacher pep talks . . . and study the Bible myself?

Do I really need church? Why?

I need church because it is a hospital.

I may *feel* fine, but if I were diagnosed with an internal tumor I would seek treatment fast. The other option would be to check out a surgery textbook from the nearby medical library, buy some razor blades and a bottle of whiskey . . . and operate on myself. The directions would be right there in the book, sort of. But I'd carve myself into hamburger before I made sense out of the medical lingo and references.

Instead, I would place myself in the care of a trained specialist who has studied the textbook extensively—someone who knows a lot more than I about muscle tissue, veins, nerves, organ functions, and suturing. The operation would take place in a hospital, where my surgeon would be helped by assistants, an anesthetist, a scrub nurse, and a circulating nurse. Nearby would be some surgical technicians and aides—all well trained and generally understanding of their patient's needs.

When you're admitted to a hospital, you are surrounded by a strange wonderland of sights, smells, and feelings. They don't serve Big Macs at dinner and the nurses don't wear jeans. Everything is a bit formal, and you can get to feeling uneasy. But a comforting thought is that a hospital is a place where sick people gather for one purpose: to have their health restored. It's a place to be examined and cared for by trained experts; a place to find comfort from those who have faced similar operations and illnesses; and a place where you, too, can comfort others as you recover.

As head of the church and Chief Physician, Jesus Christ has diagnosed us all with a terminal illness called sin. Thankfully, he has established a "hospital for sinners."

See also: Psalm 147:3; Luke 5:27–32

IN MEMORIAM

> *The Lord Jesus, on the night he was betrayed, took bread, and when he had given thanks, he broke it and said, "This is my body, which is for you; do this in remembrance of me." In the same way, after supper he took the cup, saying, "This cup is the new covenant in my blood; do this, whenever you drink it, in remembrance of me." For whenever you eat this bread and drink this cup, you proclaim the Lord's death until he comes.*

> 1 CORINTHIANS 11:23–26

Why bother with church? If worship is a private matter between me and God, then why all the fuss and public pageantry? Do I really need to cram my body into a crowded pew every Sunday or participate in rituals such as communion?

Do I really need church? Why?

I need church because it is a memorial service.

Imagine that I had been driving down a lazy country road when I lost control of the car and rolled it, end over end, into a ditch. A passerby spotted the wreckage and pulled me free . . . just as the car exploded, killing him instantly. A few days later, a memorial service is held for the man. Would I go? Of course.

The Bible says that Christ was God's sacrifice for me—that Jesus stepped between me and death. And when I attend church, it's a way of remembering that. I could, of course, observe a moment of silence while lying in bed or during a commercial break on TV. I could just sing a hymn in the shower or read a psalm on my way to the store. But I think God deserves more than that.

A memorial service is intended to be a group affair. "Let us not give up meeting together, as some are in the habit of doing," the author of Hebrews wrote to a band of young believers. By drawing together weekly and by taking communion, we share in a common experience and inspire one another to greater enthusiasm toward God.

That spirit of worship cannot be captured in the same way when I'm stretched out in bed with the covers yanked tight around my shoulders.

As head of the church, Jesus Christ has invited us to his memorial service. He died for us, and he doesn't want us to forget that act of love.

See also: Hebrews 10:25; 2 Timothy 2:8

IN TRAINING

Train yourself to be godly.

1 TIMOTHY 4:7

Why bother with church? I don't have much in common with others who attend. Besides, going to church doesn't make me a Christian any more than going to a bank makes me rich. Am I not safe as long as I've invited Christ into my heart and asked his forgiveness for sin?

Do I really need church? Why?

I need church because it is a training camp.

When I rowed for my university crew team, there was a fellow teammate who often ducked practice. "Gee, Coach, I jammed my finger playing volleyball yesterday," he said one morning as the rest of us were suiting up and gathering our oars. The following week he said he'd hurt his leg sliding into second during an intramural softball game. Other times he couldn't work out with the team because he had to work ... or fix his car ... or take someone to the airport.

His well-timed excuses were basically just cover-ups. He wanted the glory of "being on the team." But he wanted it the easy way—without having to train.

Church is like team practice—a training camp where Christians learn how to be better ... well, better *Christians*. I can duck practice, but I'm no good to the team when I do. Like my teammates, I am preparing for a race that will last my entire life—a race that involves following a course established some 2,000 years ago when Christ paved the path that leads to God.

"Train yourself to be godly," Paul wrote to Timothy. When I was born, no one had to train me to be bad. Smearing mustard on the wall and stuffing beans up my nose came naturally. But godliness doesn't "just happen," like an athlete doesn't "just happen" to pole vault eighteen feet or run a four-minute mile. It comes with training—learning the fundamentals and then perfecting them with the help and encouragement of other teammates.

As head of the church, Jesus Christ has called us to join him at training camp. There's a big race ahead, and he wants us to be prepared for it.

See also: Luke 6:40; 1 Corinthians 9:24–27; 1 Timothy 4:8

POINTS TO PONDER—CHURCH

Be shepherds of the church of God, which he bought with his own blood.

ACTS 20:28

You aren't too bad to come in. You aren't too good to stay out.

CHURCH BULLETIN BOARD

Our great-grandfathers called it the holy Sabbath; our grandfathers, the Sabbath; our fathers, Sunday; but today we call it the weekend.

WESLEYAN METHODIST

God never intended his church to be a refrigerator in which to preserve perishable piety. He intended it to be an incubator in which to hatch converts.

F. LINCICOME

The holiest moment of the church service is the moment when God's people—strengthened by preaching and sacrament—go out of the church door into the world to be *the Church*. We don't *go* to church; we *are* the Church.

ERNEST SOUTHCOTT

When Christian worship is dull and joyless, Jesus Christ has been left outside—that is the only possible explanation.

JAMES S. STEWART

The birth and rapid rise of the Christian Church remain an unsolved enigma for any historian who refuses to take seriously the only explanation offered by the Church itself.

C. F. D. MOULE

Don't stay away from church because there are so many hypocrites. There's always room for one more.

ARTHUR R. ADAMS

Tell me what the young of England are doing on Sunday, and I will tell you what the future of England will be.

WILLIAM E. GLADSTONE

Jesus spoke about the ox in the ditch on the Sabbath. But if your ox gets in the ditch every Sabbath, you should either get rid of the ox or fill up the ditch.

BILLY GRAHAM

You see, God, it's like this: We could attend church more faithfully if your day came at some other time. You have chosen a day that comes at the end of a hard week, and we're all tired out. Not only that, but it's the day following Saturday night, and Saturday night is one time when we feel that we should go out and enjoy ourselves. Often it is after midnight when we reach home, and it is impossible to get up on Sunday morning. We'd like to go to church, and know we should; but you have just chosen the wrong day.

TWENTIETH CENTURY CHRISTIAN

When I first became a Christian . . . I thought that I could do it on my own, by retiring to my rooms and reading theology, and I wouldn't go to the churches and Gospel Halls; . . . I disliked very much their hymns, which I considered to be fifth-rate poems set to sixth-rate music. But as I went on I saw the great merit of it. I came up against different people of quite different outlooks and different education, and then gradually my conceit just began peeling off. I realized that the hymns (which were just sixth-rate music) were, nevertheless, being sung with devotion and benefit by an old saint in elastic-side boots in the opposite pew, and then you realize that you aren't fit to clean those boots. It gets you out of your solitary conceit.

C. S. LEWIS

See also: Acts 2:42; 1 Corinthians 12:27; Hebrews 10:25

WEEK

22

LIMBO

Because you are lukewarm – neither hot nor cold –
I am about to spit you out of my mouth.

REVELATION 3:16

A couple of months after I became a Christian, Rachel invited me to a party at her place. We'd met at a Bible study a few weeks earlier, and she seemed like a fun person to get to know.

By the time I arrived, cars snaked down both sides of her street. I parked at the end of the line, behind a Toyota with a couple necking in the backseat. Not knowing what a "Christian" party was like, I stuck a small Bible in my pocket just in case.

My knock at the door couldn't be heard above the music, so I finally just walked in. When I entered, Rachel staggered toward me through a blue haze of cigarette smoke.

"Well, if it isn't Misser Chrishun!" she said through a crooked, silly smile. She started to tilt and I grabbed her arm. "No, no, I'm *perfely* sober. Now," she said, giving me a little push toward the kitchen, "the Bud's in there. Go get yersef lit and we'll talk s'more." I hesitated. "Go an get yersef happy. There's plenny beer!"

Months earlier, I would have felt perfectly comfortable being there. But the things I enjoyed doing changed when I became a Christian. I thought that happened to *everyone* who claimed to be a Christian. But Rachel seemed to be an exception. As soon as she turned her back, I quietly slipped out.

The following Monday I spotted her in the cafeteria and tried to explain why I'd left. "Don't be such a deadhead," she said nonchalantly. "People were just having a little fun. Besides, being a Christian doesn't mean I can't have a good time."

It was hard to figure Rachel out. She periodically continued to attend Bible studies. But I wondered what difference it made, because she reverted to being her same old self as soon as she left the meeting.

If she blew an easy tennis shot in the class we shared, she'd throw a fit that made John McEnroe seem polite. She wore her blouse open an extra button and flirted with everyone, even the bald math teacher. Whenever I passed her in the halls, she was on the arm of one of the loosest guys at school. I heard talk that she was taking the pill. That may have been rumor, but I somehow doubted it.

The odd thing is that Rachel often wore a necklace with a gold cross. I know the Bible tells us not to judge others, but I always thought it looked out of place dangling from her neck. I think to her it was just a piece of jewelry instead of a symbol of the One who died for our sins.

See also: Matthew 3:10; 7:21–23; Ephesians 4:17–5:21; 2 Timothy 3:1–5

KNOCK KNOCK ...

I am the way.

JOHN 14:6

From inside the large, elegant supper club came the sounds of laughter and fun. It was a bright, clear night—the kind of evening where the millions of stars seem to be within hand's reach, where the sidewalks seem to lead straight to the moon. On this magic night in Los Angeles, scores of couples had come to dine and dance. Music seeped beneath the doors, drifted through the windows, and seemed to enliven all that passed by outside.

Suddenly, the merriment turned to horror. Smoke and flames poured from the lobby. The dining area was enveloped in a dark, choking cloud. The only light came from the flashing orange tongues that licked at the walls and ceiling. Patrons scrambled from their chairs, screaming, and stampeded for the side exits.

A clot of people fought to get to the same doors. Panic ensued. Those felled by the smoke and fire were trampled. People climbed over bodies, pushing and shoving to get outside. But through the din of cries and wails came the horrific scream, "THE DOORS ARE LOCKED!"

Those who saw this story in the newspaper probably just skimmed a few paragraphs, felt a pang of incredulity, and then forgot it. Similar catastrophes happen so frequently that we are desensitized—especially when we don't know any of the dead. But the disaster stuck in my mind, perhaps because it reminded me of another closed-door tragedy that I see happening all around me. The difference is, my friends and family are among the victims.

You see, Jesus Christ is the doorway to God. He left no doubt about it: "No one comes to the Father except through me." On another occasion he added: "If anyone enters through me, he shall be saved." On this matter, Christ was *dead* serious.

To put it quite literally, he went to hell and back to open heaven's door and pave the way for us to forgiveness of sin, closeness with God, and eternal life. And even though people reject that claim and slam the door in his face, yet he stands there patiently knocking. Rather, patiently *pounding*. At stake is a matter of life and death.

See also: Matthew 7:8; Luke 12:35–36; John 6:37; Revelation 3:20

POSSIBILITY BELIEVING

Everything is possible for him who believes.

MARK 9:23

Christ made this statement when a man approached him with his son, who was possessed with some kind of an evil spirit. The spirit had turned the boy into a neighborhood freak, a circus sideshow of sorts.

As the boy stood face-to-face with Jesus, surrounded by a large crowd, he flopped on the ground and started writhing about like a fish out of water. Foam from his mouth mingled with dust to form a dark, dirty pool. His rigid legs beat the earth like drumsticks. It must have been some sight; you can imagine the bystanders gawking and whispering to each other.

"If you can do anything, take pity on us and help us," the man said to Christ, ignoring the crush of people.

"'*If* you can'?" replied Jesus. "Everything is possible for him who believes."

Christ didn't say everything is possible if you run with the right crowd, kneel when you pray, and wear designer togas. He didn't say all is possible if you're a premed student at Jerusalem U., tithe your shekels to First Central Synagogue in Nazareth, or know how to win friends and influence people. The only prerequisite was simply that the man *believe* Christ could turn his "impossibility" into a possibility.

"I do believe," the man immediately blurted. "Help me overcome my unbelief!" His lingering doubt vanished quickly when Christ did exactly that and healed his son.

"If you have faith as small as a mustard seed," Christ later told his disciples, "you can say to this mountain, 'Move from here to there' and it will move." Close your eyes a moment and think about the mountains in your life—the impossible and sometimes unbelievable situations facing you—that need to be moved.

Perhaps it's a haunting memory of past sin, a wrong relationship, or a problem at home. Perhaps it's a crippling feeling of inferiority or a nagging worry about your future. These "mountains" are what Charles Swindoll calls "great opportunities brilliantly disguised as impossible situations."

The "opportunity" is to allow God enough elbowroom in your life to do what he's best at: turning your impossibilities into possibilities. Listen to Jeremiah's words: "Ah, Sovereign Lord, you have made the heavens and the earth by your great power and outstretched arm. *Nothing is too hard for you.*"

Moving mountains is not something to tackle on your own. No chance of budging them an inch if you think you can do the job alone. Every chance in the world if you trust God to do it.

See also: Jeremiah 32:17; Proverbs 3:5–6; Luke 1:37; 18:27

THE BOX

Be very careful, then, how you live—not as unwise but as wise, making the most of every opportunity, because the days are evil. Therefore do not be foolish, but understand what the Lord's will is.

EPHESIANS 5:15–17

Sitting in a sauna is basically a passive experience. Blasts of steam envelop your body, making you sweat as if you've just returned from a long run on a hot summer day. In a sense, a sauna tricks your body: it creates feelings associated with having done something when you really have done nothing.

Watching television works basically on the same principle. It washes your mind with sights and sounds that create the feeling of "being there." A program about whitewater rafting, for example, will make it seem like you're actually in the bucking boat. But when the commercial blinks on, you realize you've been duped. You're actually doing nothing—just sitting in a room staring at a box.

Studies indicate the average American youth spends between twenty and twenty-four hours a week watching a piece of furniture crack jokes, tell stories, relay news, and otherwise entertain. That's about three to four hours a day—one-fifth of your waking hours. In small doses, TV may help you relax and get your mind off hassles at school, home, or work. But after a certain point, you must ask yourself: "What am I *not* doing during the time I spend watching TV?"

Because television is a recent invention, the Bible says nothing about it—just as it doesn't mention Ford Mustangs, Bazooka bubble gum, or McDonald's. But it has much to say about what we fill our minds with and how we use our time. In Ephesians 5:15–17 the apostle Paul indicates that these last days are evil days. The Lord's return is near. Each day is therefore extremely valuable. We shouldn't squander our hours. He says we should live wisely, "making the most of every opportunity" to do good and be about God's business.

Someday soon we will all face God and be asked to give an account for our lives. How about you? Will you have something to show? Or will the story of your life read like pages from *TV Guide?*

See also: Romans 14:12; 12:2; Philippians 3:14–21

DAY BY DAY

Give us today our daily bread.

MATTHEW 6:11

One of Thomas Carlyle's most ambitious works, a book on the French Revolution, took two years to write. The day he finished, he gave the only copy of the manuscript to a friend and fellow writer, John Stuart Mill, to read and critique.

Several days later, Mill raced back to Carlyle's home in a frenzy. He pounded on the front door like a crazy man. "I-I don't know what to say or how to apologize," he stammered, and then told how his dim-witted housegirl had used the manuscript as kindling to start a fire.

No answer from Carlyle—just a glazed, empty stare. When the extent of the tragedy sunk in, his face paled. He hung on the door for support. Two full years of his life were lost. The thousands of long, lonely hours spent writing were wasted. It was the worst nightmare he could imagine. How could he possibly write the book again? The thought paralyzed him, and he lapsed into one of the deepest, darkest depressions of his life.

Then one day, as he was walking the streets to gather his mind and seek some direction for his life, he stopped to watch the construction of a massive stone wall. Carlyle was transfixed. That tall, sweeping wall was being raised one stone at a time.

He knew what he had to do. "I'll just write one page at a time. One page today, one page tomorrow—that's all I will think about."

When faced with seemingly impossible situations, we often see the wall and not the individual stones. Perhaps you're overwhelmed by the demands from your teachers, your boss, your parents. As a whole, the load can seemingly break you. But taken day by day, task by task, the load is manageable.

The same is true of spiritual matters. You can feel boggled reading the Bible because God's expectations are a mile long. Take them instead one by one. Worry less about attaining God's plan for your *life* . . . just work on *today*. Godly character is built by laying stone on stone, minute by minute, day by day, in a thousand small, seemingly insignificant ways. Give your entire attention to what God is doing right now.

Let Christ be your example. He prayed for *daily* bread, *daily* sustenance. He knew tomorrow would take care of itself.

See also: Joshua 1:9; Proverbs 27:1; Matthew 6:25–34; 1 Corinthians 10:13

ONE-NIGHT STANDS

Just as you received Christ Jesus as Lord, continue to live in him, rooted and built up in him, strengthened in the faith as you were taught, and overflowing with thankfulness.

COLOSSIANS 2:6–7

The way some people talk, becoming a Christian is hardly more involved than mixing a bowl of instant oatmeal. They speak of being born again, and can circle dates on calendars. But if you check with many of them after a few months or years, you'll likely find their warm, mushy feelings about God have cooled.

"It just didn't work," they'll say with a shrug, as if the directions on the box were bad.

A recent Gallup Poll showed that some 50 million Americans claim to have had a dramatic, one-time encounter with God. With all of the trouble in the world, I suspect that "being on God's side" somehow made them feel safer. The same Gallup Poll concluded with these shocking words: "Religious experience is on the increase; morality is on the decrease."

That's odd. Shouldn't a confrontation with God cause an upswing in morality? Or is it just that one-night stands with God have no life-changing impact?

Becoming an instant Christian makes as much sense as becoming an instant surgeon. Dr. Christiaan Barnard didn't just pick up a scalpel and suddenly start transplanting hearts. Nor can you arrive overnight as a Christian. In Romans 6, 7, and 8, Paul describes the constant struggles Christians face—it's as if we have civil wars raging in our hearts. Winning those battles takes *time*.

In his letter to the Colossians, Paul speaks about being *rooted*, *strengthened*, *built up* in faith. Salvation, like corn, doesn't sprout overnight. If it's true and healthy, it must be nurtured, weeded, watered, fertilized. It is a loving *process* of drawing closer to God.

As you read yesterday, lasting change is built by laying stone on stone. It takes work, risk, dedication, sacrifice ... and especially time. God rushes no one, and expects instant saints of none.

See also: Galatians 6:7–9; Ephesians 3:14–21; Hebrews 3:14

SHUT OUT

> *Peter said to Jesus, "Lord, it is good for us to be here. If you wish, I will put up three shelters—one for you, one for Moses and one for Elijah."*
>
> #### MATTHEW 17:4

He was the ultimate mystery man—so reclusive that getting a picture of him was like trying to get a formal portrait of Bigfoot. During his later years, he never saw outsiders, so his appearance was unimportant to him. His hair and scraggly beard curled halfway to the floor. His nails were long and twisted, like two-inch corkscrews. He seldom bathed.

A skid row bum? No, Howard Hughes—one of the wealthiest men in the world before his death in 1976.

Why was he so enigmatic, so isolated? His closest aides reported that Hughes simply wanted to keep his environment sanitized, to maintain germproof sterility. People carried disease, so he locked them out. But he died from disease anyway—the *loneliness* disease.

The Howard Hughes story reminds me somewhat of Peter, who one afternoon hiked up a high mountain with Jesus and two other disciples. Upon reaching the summit, something strange happened. While Jesus was praying, Matthew reports, his face shone like the sun, and his clothes became as white as light. Mark, who today could make a killing doing Clorox commercials, says Jesus' clothes dazzled as if he'd used supernatural bleach. Moments later, Jesus was joined by Moses and Elijah.

Peter's toes tingled so much he couldn't contain himself. "Lord," he blurted, "isn't it great we're here!" Translation: "Thank God it's *us* and no one else." And then he volunteered to construct a mountain lodge so they wouldn't have to leave the holy peak. They could stay there and have a male bonding experience—apart from people and the dirt of their problems. It would be germproof living.

Jesus didn't answer him. But God did. Speaking from a cloud, he boomed that the wisest thing Peter could do was to zip his lip. And that scared Peter so badly he fell on his face and nearly knocked himself out.

In each of us is a touch of both Howard Hughes and Peter. We hoard our privacy, hiding behind locked doors—and not just physical ones. We shut people out as easily with harsh words and looks. The same is true when we hang out in cliques or post those invisible banners: "SENIORS ONLY" or "WHITES ONLY" or "CHRISTIANS ONLY." We don't want to get *too* involved in others' problems or lives. There are times when, as Mark Twain said, we'd like to hang the whole human race, and finish the farce.

But isolation is anathema to Christianity, which was built on relationship. That's why Christ admonished his followers to be the salt of the earth. To do the job right, salt can't stay in the shaker.

See also: Matthew 25:31–46; Luke 10:25–37; Hebrews 10:25

W E E K 23

GUILT THAT KILLS

Let us then approach the throne of grace with confidence, so that we may receive mercy and find grace to help us in our time of need.

HEBREWS 4:16

It was late summer, during the lull that precedes the start of school. Bobby, 18, and his 16-year-old girlfriend, Joanne, were on their way to visit friends. But before they arrived, Bobby fell asleep at the wheel and smashed into an 18-wheel truck, killing Joanne instantly. Bobby escaped with bruises.

Knowing he was to blame for Joanne's death, Bobby asked God to forgive him. But that seemed too easy. And Bobby wanted others to know how sorry he felt. So a few weeks after Joanne's funeral, he borrowed a gun and shot himself.

Bobby's suicide a few years ago reminded me of the story of the man riding down the road on a donkey, carrying a 200-pound sack of wheat on his shoulders.

"Why don't you take the weight off your shoulders and put it on the donkey?" asked a passerby.

"You don't think," the man responded, "that I'd ask the donkey to carry all that weight, do you?"

Because we're imperfect human beings, we'll never be free from the weight of guilt. It's there to remind us when we fall short of God's standards. Yet God is not some cosmic madman who delights in watching us squirm. He makes it very clear that he wants to remove the burden from our shoulders and give rest to the weary.

But people respond to guilt in different ways. Take Judas and Peter, for example. Both were trusted disciples, yet both turned on Christ. Judas betrayed him to a crowd of thugs and Hebrew zealots, leading to Christ's capture. And then when Christ was on trial for his life, Peter denied three times even knowing him. Both men were overwhelmed with guilt.

Judas wanted to advertise how sorry he felt, so he hung himself. On the other hand, Peter resolved his guilt before God and went on to become the key disciple in spreading the news of Christ.

Our reactions to guilt may not be as dramatic as were Bobby's, Judas's, or Peter's. But our response can either drive us further from God or closer to him. The Bible makes it clear that God prefers the latter. He only asks that we admit our need and trust him with the load. And then we can walk in newness of life—precious, free, forgiven life.

See also: Jeremiah 31:25; Matthew 11:28; John 7:37

COACH BILL

> *It is God who works in you to will and to act according to his good purpose.*
>
> PHILIPPIANS 2:13

When I rowed for my college crew team, I awoke six mornings a week to a jangling alarm clock set for 4:30. I was never much of a morning person, but I didn't have much to say about the matter. It was all part of the training regimen set by the coach.

Coach Bill wanted team members up with the street sweepers and on the water by 5:00 for a grueling two-hour workout before classes. He also required that we spend an hour pumping iron and that we run ten miles daily—the last thing I often felt like doing. All of my friends would be having fun, and I'd be out there sweating to death.

Sometimes I'd talk to Coach Bill about the frustrations I felt because of the stiff training schedule or about the searing pain I felt in my legs from shin splints I developed from pounding the pavement each day. Coach Bill never bawled me out for feeling that way. Rather, he'd lace up his running shoes and join me for a jog. You see, he never wanted team members to feel like they were struggling on their own. He wanted us to know he was supporting us and working with us for the same goals.

That same attitude is shared by God. When I get discouraged as a Christian or feel I've fallen short of God's expectations, I take a few minutes to talk it over with him. He doesn't zap me for my shortcomings. Rather, in his ever-loving, ever-compassionate way, he assures me that I am not alone.

Through his Holy Spirit, he's at work in me—helping me to do what he wants. He doesn't set arbitrary goals and then sit back and watch me struggle. He's a hands-on God—always there to help me meet the goals.

See also: Joshua 1:5, 9; John 14:23–27

FOLLOWING THE PIPER

Here I am! I stand at the door and knock. If any-one hears my voice and opens the door, I will go in and eat with him, and he with me.

REVELATION 3:20

When I was a kid, we had several cats—adopted, for the most part, by my brother on his way home from school. They'd follow him like the Pied Piper, though I suspect he carried catnip in his hip pocket.

Most of the cats were fat and lazy, with the personality of a pillow. But one tagalong was an alley brawler whose eerie banshee screams kept the neighborhood awake at night. I became fairly used to him dragging home from his back-lot prize fights with a little less fur and a few more holes in his right ear. It's like when you live with someone day after day, you don't notice them gaining or losing weight. The tom was losing parts of his body, but at a slow rate. So I paid little attention until a friend commented, "That cat of yours is sure falling apart."

Our lives as Christians can fall apart like that in ways we hardly notice. God is not first in our lives. He's not even fifth or sixth or thirteenth. He trails the pack of our priorities. We may be vaguely aware that we've taken that slow, downhill slide from God. We may even wake up at night, try to stare down the ceiling, and attempt to determine what went wrong. But "what went wrong" occurred so slowly we thought we were somehow still right. We have lost our joy, happiness, and hope—great hunks of our beings as Christians—yet keep on living as if everything is fine. We don't realize we're in hot water.

Some mad biologist with a penchant for the perverse conducted an experiment in which he put a number of frogs in a pot of water and very, very slowly heated the water to a boil. They could have easily hopped out, but the change in temperature occurred so slowly that none seemed to notice. In the end, every frog died.

We're that way, too. At any time we're free to turn back to God, to seek his help in overcoming the sin and habits and worries that bog us down. "Come unto me," he says, arms open wide. Yet we're slow to embrace his forgiveness and experience healing.

As Christians, we seldom truly wrestle with Satan's powers as we should. We've joined them. We've dropped into line and are following the Piper. Is it too late to stand apart, to renew that fresh joy, to experience the purpose of life you once had? *Never.*

"Here I am! I stand at the door and knock," Christ says. You opened the door once. Go ahead—open it to him again.

See also: Isaiah 1:18; Romans 12:2; Hebrews 10:15–17

HIT OR MISS

All Scripture is God-breathed and is useful for teaching, rebuking, correcting and training in righteousness.

2 TIMOTHY 3:16

Perhaps you've heard the story of the young student who wanted to know God's will for his future. So he took his Bible, opened it at random, closed his eyes, and dropped his finger to the page—assuming that the verse it came to rest on would be God's way of directing his future steps.

To his dismay, his finger fell on Matthew 27:5, which says Judas "went away and hanged himself." The young man tried again, and his finger landed on Luke 10:37: "Go and do likewise." Following the same procedure a third time, his finger pointed to John 13:27: "What you are about to do, do quickly."

The point is clear. You're liable to get the wrong message if you treat Scripture like fortune cookies. But that's what many people do. Instead of reading the Bible in some systematic fashion, they expect good-luck passages to pop out. Or they hunt and peck for God's will in a hit-or-miss manner. And they generally miss more than they hit. Others read only their favorite passages—sticking to the verses they particularly like. But balanced spiritual growth doesn't happen from a milk-and-Twinkies pattern of reading Scripture. Dig into the meat!

Paul says to Timothy that *all* Scripture is God-breathed. In other words, the writers of the Bible didn't just dream up good and challenging thoughts as if writing clever sayings for greeting cards. They penned what the Holy Spirit directed them to write. Because of that the Bible is like no other book in existence. It is God's owner's manual for the planet Earth. By dissecting it word by word, we can learn how to live life to his full, complete specifications. I think that's sort of what Timothy means when he says *all* of the Bible is *useful*.

It's like the owner's manual for your car. Just reading about how to change the oil won't help you if your carburetor or fuel pump is bad. In the same way, the Bible can help in every area of our lives by *teaching* (educating us about the nature of God, for example), *rebuking* (reprimanding us for wrong behavior), *correcting* (helping us adjust our behavior to God's standards), and *training in righteousness* (instructing us on *how* we can live as God intends).

If all of the Bible is inspired by God, we should read it all. But beyond that, we must let it permeate our lives to the point that we *act* on what we read. "Do not merely listen to the word," writes the apostle James. "Do what it says."

Being a "doer of the word" is not just an idle suggestion. It's the Lord's directive for a truly God-breathed way of living.

See also: Psalm 119:1–16; James 1:21–25

OWNER'S MANUAL

> *Your word is a lamp to my feet and a light for my path.*
>
> PSALM 119:105

Twin borders of white lights stretch the distance of the runway, forming a fluorescent path for planes as they scream down from the darkness and brake for a safe landing. On a clear night, a pilot can see the beacons for miles. They light his way, indicating where he should direct his plane. If he follows the guide lights and stays within their boundaries, all will be well. But if he strays to the right or left, outside the illuminated zone, disaster awaits.

As Christians, we have guiding lights of our own: a best-selling collection of books that mark our boundaries and illumine our path to God. These books, collectively known as the Bible, are God's "Owner's Manual" for the human race. They contain his specs on keeping the human machine tuned correctly and running smoothly.

The Bible is not, however, a technical manual of schematic diagrams and charts, nor a cold, dead, dated document. It's at once a love story, autobiography, biography, self-help text, poetry anthology, compilation of personal letters, songbook, log of genealogy, how-to manual, and collection of prophecy.

It contains testaments from men and women who have trusted God completely—providing guidance and inspiration for you—and details life histories of people who have just as completely disregarded God—giving you fair warning.

Above all, the Bible is God's way of stepping out of the shadows and making himself known. It tells us exactly what he's like, what he expects of us, why things aren't like they ought to be, and what he intends to do about it.

You think it's awful that your father died of a heart attack? So does God: He promises one day to rid the world of death and dry every tear. You think it's unfair that people can cheat and swindle their way to success? So does God: He promises that no sin or sinner will escape his judgment.

Finally, the Bible is God's word—his final word on how to experience a full, rich, abundant life. It guides you out of darkness, and it helps you maneuver through every difficulty of life, whether it's your fears about next year or your tears about a broken relationship. God knows and cares about these matters and more. You've got his word on it.

See also: Psalm 119:1–16; 2 Timothy 3:16

EYEWITNESS REPORTS

That which was from the beginning, which we have heard, which we have seen with our eyes, which we have looked at and our hands have touched—this we proclaim concerning the Word of life.

1 JOHN 1:1

When Pan Am's flight 759 crashed on takeoff from New Orleans a few years ago, reporters rushed to interview witnesses. "I saw the belly of it," said one passerby of the doomed 727. "It was spitting and popping like it couldn't get the motor running." A neighbor added, "There was a wall of flame all across the street. I thought I was in hell."

Sometimes, when the event that has been experienced is important or newsworthy enough, the witnesses will write books about it. Presidents often publish their memoirs of history. And close friends of famous personalities often write "insider accounts." What was Elvis or Hitler or Babe Ruth really like? All you have to do is read the book.

If you want to know more about Christ, all you have to do is open your Bible—a library of books written, for the most part, by his closest followers. Writing independently, Matthew, Mark, Luke, and John documented the events of Christ's life scene by scene. Did Jesus *really* raise Lazarus from death? Did he *really* heal the blind, rebuke religious leaders, and forgive sinners? Did he *really* say we are immortal creatures and claim to be the Son of God? You have the words of four separate writers.

As John wrote in his gospel: "These [things] are written that you may believe that Jesus is the Christ, the Son of God, and that by believing you may have life in his name." In his later epistles, John wanted his readers to know that his words weren't hand-me-down truths, passed to him from a friend of a friend. As one of the twelve disciples, John was an eyewitness to all that Christ did and said. That's why he opened his first epistle by saying, in effect, "I'm writing about what I know personally. I'm not making it up. Believe me—I was there with Christ!"

Unlike many authors today who ride the talk-show circuit, John and Jesus' other biographers didn't write for money or fame. They simply wrote so that others might come to know Christ as well as they did.

See also: 2 Timothy 1:12; 1 John 1:2–4; 5:13–14

POINTS TO PONDER—THE BIBLE

Don't you know what the Scripture says . . . ?

ROMANS 11:2

Most people are bothered by those passages of Scripture they do not understand, but the passages that bother me are those I do understand.

MARK TWAIN

A man who loves his wife will love her letters and her photographs because they speak to him of her. So if we love the Lord Jesus we shall love the Bible because it speaks to us of him.

JOHN R. W. STOTT

If God is a reality and the soul is a reality and you are an immortal being, what are you doing with your Bible shut?

HERRICK JOHNSON

The Bible was never intended to be a book for scholars and specialists only. From the very beginning it was intended to be everybody's book, and that is what it continues to be.

F. F. BRUCE

I thoroughly believe in a university education for both men and women; but I believe a knowledge of the Bible without a college course is more valuable than a college course without the Bible.

WILLIAM LYON PHELPS

The Bible is a window in this prison of hope, through which we look into eternity.

JOHN SULLIVAN DWIGHT

Warning: This book is habit-forming. Regular use causes loss of anxiety, decreased appetite for lying, cheating, stealing, hating. Symptoms: increased sensations of love, peace, joy, compassion.

ANONYMOUS

I study my Bible as I gather apples. First, I shake the whole tree that the ripest might fall. Then I shake each limb, and when I have shaken each limb, I shake each branch and every twig. Then I look under every leaf.

MARTIN LUTHER

The Christian feels that the tooth of time gnaws all books but the Bible. It has a pertinent relevance to every age. It has worked miracles by itself alone. It has made its way where no missionary had gone and has done the missionary's work. Centuries of experience have tested the book. It has passed through critical fires no other volume has suffered, and its spiritual truth has endured the flames and come out without so much as the *smell* of burning.

W. E. SANGSTER

If you really want some mail, read a letter from Paul.

ANONYMOUS

To read the Bible as literature is like reading *Moby Dick* as a whaling manual or *The Brothers Karamazov* for its punctuation.

FREDERICK BUECHNER

God has given us in written form a volume which spans all the human emotions, the ups, the downs, the diversity of individuals, the good with the bad, the ugly, the beautiful, the sinners, the righteous, the perverted, the saved, the lost, the poetry, the poets, the wisdom, the wise, the human stories, the reality of life, pregnant with meaning, a book in fact of truth, not pale, narrow, religious sayings. The Bible, the Word of God, is solid, human, verifiable, divine indeed.

FRANKY SCHAEFFER

See also: 2 Timothy 3:16–17

WEEK

24

ALL HEART

Love must be sincere.

ROMANS 12:9

I'm your basic All-American good guy—as nice as they come. You'd know that if you took the time to get to know me. I get along with *everyone*. Except for those who ...

Don't wash their gym clothes
Stutter when they talk
   Merge too slowly on freeways
Look greasy
    Burp in shopping malls
   Have zits on their nose
    Don't listen when I talk
    Walk with a cane
     Don't remember my birthday
     Score higher than me.

And I'm really quite compassionate. All heart, as they say. Except when it comes to ...

Fat people
Old teachers
   Beer bellies
People with warts
    Vice principals
   Braggarts
    Abortionists
    And people who shoot abortionists.

We could be very best friends. We'd get along great. I'm as supportive and loving as friends come. Except toward ...

Prudes
Faggots

Nerds
Ditzes
> *Skinheads*
> *Druggies*
>> *Holy rollers*
> *Sluts*
>> *And ... of course, bigots.*

See also: Romans 12:3; Philippians 2:3–4

A WANTED MAN

O Lord, please send someone else to do it.

EXODUS 4:13

Few of the characters mentioned in the Bible were truly great men and women. Even the star players suffered from inferiority and doubt. They felt incapable at times of trusting God.

Take Moses, for example. He's often depicted as a tough-minded, bigger-than-life, dashing leader—sort of a cross between Mel Gibson and the Pope. Yet much of his life (see Ex. 2–4) he failed miserably. He botched a murder he tried to commit secretly, fled his country in fear, married a foreigner, and bummed his living off her parents by tending their sheep.

Yet God overlooked his failure, because it was at this rock-bottom time in Moses' life that God appeared to him in the burning bush, calling him to service: "So now, go. I am sending you to Pharaoh to bring my people the Israelites out of Egypt."

When Moses heard what God wanted, he stuttered with excuses. Feelings of inferiority clawed deep in his brain. All those years scrounging off his in-laws and watching stinky sheep convinced him he was a loser.

281

"Who am I, that I should go to Pharaoh?" he said. Translation: "You want *me* to do *what?* God, you've gotta be kidding! I'm not capable." Later he blurts, "What shall I tell them? What if they do not believe me?"

God's response was apparently not good enough for Moses, because in desperation he complains, "O Lord, I have never been eloquent . . . I am slow of speech and tongue . . . O Lord, please send someone else to do it."

In effect, God hand-picked Moses for a big job. But Moses wanted to run back to the farm. He felt crippled by self-doubt and low self-esteem. Not only didn't he think he was a leader type, he also thought he talked funny.

"I will help you speak and will teach you what to say," the Lord replied.

Can you identify with Moses and his lack of confidence? Perhaps you, too, are ducking God's service or some other task because you're troubled by low self-worth. If so, you've been deceived by the devil. God is able to turn your disabilities into blessings. He's not bound by your self-imposed barriers and inabilities. What you *can't* do, God *can* do. He'll go with you, helping you speak, teaching you what to say—if for no other reason than to keep you trusting him—not yourself—day by day.

If you have any doubts, just read about the rest of Moses' life.

See also: Proverbs 3:5–6

GLIMPSES OF GOD

Truly you are a God who hides himself.

ISAIAH 45:15

I have my moments, quite frankly, when it's difficult to worship God—to *connect* with him in some meaningful way. After all, he doesn't exactly maintain a high profile. When was the last time you saw him?

I'd do something about that if I were God. I wouldn't be so shy. I'd come out of hiding every few years just to remind people I was still around and that if it was heaven they were after, they still needed to reckon with me.

Perhaps God could learn from the way they start football games at the Air Force Academy in Colorado Springs. A half dozen or so young cadets bail out of a plane circling overhead and parachute onto the fifty-yard line of the field. The refs, the players, and fans all peer skyward to watch the cadets' descent, and for good reason. The game can't begin until the last parachutist lands, because he carries the game ball. As the ball is passed to the ref, the crowd roars, and then jet fighters scream overhead, slam on their afterburners, and rocket straight up and out of sight. It's enough to make you wet your pants.

I think that's how I'd do it if I were God, except I wouldn't use a parachute and I wouldn't land. I'd free-fall headfirst, and then pull up into a hover just at the top of the stadium. I'd do the jet thing, but would catch them in midair, one in each hand. And then I'd let rip a few lightning bolts just to let people know it was really me, and boom out something like, "I am the Lord your God, and you shall worship me!"

Concerns about God's low visibility are nothing new. Job cried out in desperation, "If only I knew where to find him" (Job 23:3). King David echoed his pleas: "Why, O Lord, do you stand far off?" (Psalm 10:1). Even Philip, one of Christ's disciples, looked him square in the eye and said, "Lord, show us the Father and that will be enough for us" (John 14:8).

The Bible doesn't fully explain why God does not make a bigger deal about being God, but I suspect it's largely out of respect for us. He holds back because he knows we can handle only so much reality at a time. And so he reveals himself in man-sized glimpses: the colorful splash of sunset, the promise of spring, the comfort of his Holy Spirit, the changing expressions of a baby's face, the unity of a family, the miracle of sacrificial love, the melody of rain, the humor of a snail's face, the assurance of forgiveness ...

283

These glimpses of God are special to me, but I am not content. Deep inside me is the God-given urge to know him more fully, to have regular, audible conversations together. I would eventually like to see him close-up, to worship him face to face.

That opportunity, I believe, will one day be mine.

See also: Romans 1:20; 1 Corinthians 13:12

FIREWORKS IN REVERSE

> *Being found in appearance as a man, he humbled himself and became obedient to death – even death on a cross!*
>
> PHILIPPIANS 2:8

Imagine that you are at the fairgrounds, with a video camera cocked to record the Fourth of July fireworks. Comets of color rocket skyward, exploding against the cloud canopy like dye-filled water balloons. The hot summer air is splashed with electric blues, golds, and reds. Giant, iridescent blossoms materialize with a *boom!* out of nothing.

Whoosh-whoosh-rat-a-tat-tat. The noise is louder than World War II bombings. Your whirring camera captures all the razzle-dazzle – right to the stand-up-and-holler finale.

When you later screen your film, you try something different. You switch the projector to reverse. Great, sparkling streamers of light funnel back into their cannon-lobbed canisters. Bursts of shocking greens and radiant oranges are gathered from the horizons to become plain cardboard packages. Nobody oohs and aahs. The razzle-dazzle is gone. It is hard to get too excited about seeing fireworks in reverse.

That phrase, *fireworks in reverse*, is the classic description of Jesus' visit to earth. He could have burst on the scene with a roar and thunder, illuminating the sky with the rainbow radiance of eternity. He could have made the stars twinkle green and red and gold. He could have made a Goodyear blimp of the moon, flashing his message to the huddled masses below.

Instead, God's grandeur was funneled into the plain package of a human being. His Son was born in the stink of a backyard stable and lived in poverty. He sampled the whole of human experience—all the pains, griefs, hardships. And then he died in disgrace. Many thought the razzle-dazzle of God had simply fizzled.

Yet Christ's spark of grandeur was rekindled. On Easter morning the fireworks were lit. Harnessing the heavens, he burst his bounds. He arose from death victorious—to light our lives for eternity.

See also: 2 Corinthians 8:9; Philippians 2:5–11

NEW LIGHT

> *I am the bread of life. He who comes to me will never go hungry.*

JOHN 6:35

Yesterday you read about Jesus' visit to earth being like fireworks in reverse. The word *like* is an important word. It is often used to set up an analogy.

For example, I might say I have a hoarse voice. An analogy to describe the same thing might be: My voice sounds *like* the busted gearbox of an old Jeep.

The Bible is full of analogies and figurative speech. Christ often spoke that way himself: "I am the bread of life." He meant he was *like* bread in that he provides spiritual sustenance to believers. Elsewhere he said: "You are the salt of the earth," and "You are the light of the world." He meant that you are *like* salt and light.

Writers of the Bible also frequently used analogies to describe God and their relationship to him. For example, King David wrote that God was *like* a shepherd who "makes me lie down in green pastures" and "leads me beside quiet waters."

Take a few minutes to think of some fresh analogies of your own that describe your feelings about Jesus, God, and his Word—and then write a phrase or two about why that analogy is fitting. For instance, you might say: Christ is *like* a master mechanic, because he has all the right tools to tune my life to his specs. Try a few yourself:

Jesus Christ is like _____

_____

because _____

_____

The Bible is like _____

_____

because _____

_____

God's love for me is like _____

_____

because _____

_____

See also: Psalm 19; John 10:11

THE MISSING BODY

On the first day of the week, very early in the morning, the women took the spices they had prepared and went to the tomb. They found the stone rolled away from the tomb, but when they entered, they did not find the body of the Lord Jesus.

LUKE 24:1–3

Consider for a moment that Christ did *not* rise from death; that his resurrection story is a fraud. Hoax or not, you must still explain away the empty tomb. Here are the three most probable and popular theories:

The disciples stole the body. This was the explanation first circulated by Christ's opponents. Matthew 28:11–15 records how the chief priests bribed the Roman tomb guards and had them say the disciples stole the body while they were sleeping. The problem here is that all of the disciples (except for Judas and John) later died martyr deaths for their ongoing evangelism. Put yourself in their shoes. You'd face a torturous death willingly only for something you absolutely believed to be true, even if it were actually false. You'd never die for what you knew to be a deliberate lie.

The authorities stole the body. Trouble is, it was the authorities (both Jewish and Roman) who most wanted to snuff out the hysterical claims of Christ and his followers. Killing Jesus was the first step. To drive the last nail in the coffin of Christianity, they could simply have paraded his stinky corpse down Jerusalem Boulevard a week or so after his "Resurrection." That they didn't do this indicates they didn't have the body.

Christ never really died. This theory supposes that Christ entered a coma-like state after the Crucifixion and was mistakenly reported dead. He later revived in the tomb, removed the massive boulder, escaped the guards, and faked resurrection to his disciples and others. Be serious. How would *you* feel after being beaten, whipped, nailed to a cross, stabbed in the side, and entombed for three days without food or water?

Even the German critic David Strauss rejected this idea: "It is impossible that one who had just come forth from the grave, half dead, who crept about weak and ill in need of medical treatment, could ever have given the disciples the impression that he was a conqueror over death; that he was the Prince of Life. Such a resuscitation could by no possibility have changed their sorrow into enthusiasm or elevated their reverence into worship."

There's only one theory that adequately explains the empty tomb: that Christ was truly resurrected from the dead, as recorded in Scripture. You can stake your life on it.

See also: 1 Corinthians 15; 1 Thessalonians 4:13–18

POINTS TO PONDER–THE RESURRECTION

He has risen!

LUKE 24:6

Since that Sunday dawn when the tomb of Jesus was first discovered to be empty, much has been written about that day and Jesus' resurrection. Some of those statements are worth pondering: The stone was rolled away from the door, not to permit Christ to come out, but to enable the disciples to go in.

PETER MARSHALL

The biggest fact about Joseph's tomb was that it wasn't a tomb at all–it was a room for a transient. Jesus stopped there a night or two on his way back to glory.

HERBERT BOOTH SMITH

I danced on a Friday
When the sky turned black;
It's hard to dance
With the devil on your back.
They buried my body
And they thought I'd gone;
But I am the dance and I still go on:
Dance, then, wherever you may be;
I am the Lord of the Dance, said he.

And I'll lead you all, wherever you may be,
And I'll lead you all in the dance, said he.

SYDNEY CARTER, SONG

Jesus blew everything apart, and when I saw where the pieces landed I knew I was free.

GEORGE FOSTER

The birth and rapid rise of the Christian Church remain an unsolved enigma for any historian who refuses to take seriously the only explanation offered by the church itself.

C. F. D. MOULE

The Gospels do not explain the resurrection; the resurrection explains the Gospels. Belief in the resurrection is not an appendage to the Christian faith; it *is* the Christian faith.

JOHN S. WHALE

You can't keep a good man down.

FOLK SAYING

The only shadow on the cloudless Easter day of God's victory is the poverty of my own devotion, the memory of ineffective hours of unbelief, and my own stingy response to God's generosity.

A. E. WHITHAM

The Easter Bunny never rose again.

S. RICKLY CHRISTIAN

Our Lord has written the promise of the resurrection, not in books alone, but in every leaf in springtime.

MARTIN LUTHER

See also: John 20–21; Acts 26:8; 1 Corinthians 15:14–32

WEEK

25

INFANT DOE

> *You created my inmost being; you knit me together
> in my mother's womb. I praise you because I am fearfully
> and wonderfully made; your works are wonderful, I know
> that full well. My frame was not hidden from you when I
> was made in the secret place. When I was woven together
> in the depths of the earth, your eyes saw my unformed
> body. All the days ordained for me were written in your
> book before one of them came to be.*

> PSALM 139:13–16

The birth of "Infant Doe" was different than yours or mine. The parents didn't smile. Nor did they want to hold their child. They asked the doctor to take the infant away.

That's because the child wasn't like what they had expected. It would never be an athlete or have a Mensa IQ. Born with a physical handicap, the baby would require surgery to allow food to reach its stomach. But the parents refused to sign the consent form. Instead, they let their child starve to death.

This is no make-believe story. It happened a few years ago in Bloomington, Indiana. Rather than save their child, they chose "treatment to do nothing"—legal gobbledygook allowing them to get rid of their burden by killing it.

For "Infant Doe," being unwanted was a capital offense.

You might think this is an isolated case. It's not. A $350 million abortion industry has developed in this country alone, destroying more than one million babies every year. And in many cases, the killing occurs *after* birth when doctors withhold either needed medical treatment or food—as in the case of the Bloomington baby.

Being unwanted is a dreadful thing. Of course, "Infant Doe" didn't know that, because he was too young to realize the horror of his own death. But each time such a child dies, God surely cringes.

We should, too, because fellow human beings daily declare "unfit to live" those whom God has "fearfully and wonderfully made." It's a lot like what happened in Nazi Germany.

The only reason Nazis got away with their atrocities was because good people did nothing. The same thing is happening here today.

See also: Genesis 1:27; Deuteronomy 5:17

EVERY YEAR A NEW LEG

Now we ask you, brothers, to respect those who work hard among you, who are over you in the Lord and who admonish you. Hold them in the highest regard in love because of their work. Live in peace with each other.

1 Thessalonians 5:12–13

It was sometimes hard to tell that Pat Vance had a handicap. But there were a few dead giveaways. At the start of every school year he would freak out the new kids by reaching down to adjust his shoe, and then suddenly wrench his leg around backward. Or in gym, he would kick a ball and, on impact, send his leg flying in a dizzy arch. He liked the laughs that got.

Though born with a birth defect that resulted in the amputation of his right leg, Pat says he never felt unusual growing up. He credits his dad for that. In fact, things could have been horrible were it not for his father.

That's because when Pat arrived home after his amputation, his dad quit his job as a space engineer and worked without pay for a year with a maker of artificial limbs. Why? So his son wouldn't have to walk on a crude factory-made prosthesis.

Year after year he tooled and tinkered, experimented with fiberglass and resins, and baked the finished designs in the kitchen

293

oven, filling the house with terrible fumes. He built an entire work-shop, just to craft improved legs for Pat. And many nights he worked around the clock to perfect a new model—or a bigger model when his son outgrew the old.

Like most teens, Pat was never really close with his father. His dad was 52 when Pat was born, and always seemed reserved. They had the typical hassles, and sometimes Pat took his dad's absence of emotion for a lack of love. But then one day he got to thinking about how easy it is to get hung up on the "warm fuzzies" side of love and forget that parents show their love in many, very different ways.

"Sometimes it's through cleaning up after their kids have vomited," he said. "Sometimes it's through letting their kids go out with people they really don't approve of or through paying for college when they really want you to go to another school. In my case it's obvious how Dad showed his love to me. I can see the proof in file drawers full of designs and blueprints of my legs. He's in his '70s now, still working, hoping to come up with an improved version next year."

As Pat discovered, a parent's loving actions *do* speak louder than words.

See also: 1 Corinthians 13:1; Colossians 3:20; 1 John 3:18

GOODNESS, ME?

At just the right time, when we were still powerless, Christ died for the ungodly. Very rarely will anyone die for a righteous man, though for a good man someone might possibly dare to die. But God demonstrates his own love for us in this: While we were still sinners, Christ died for us.

ROMANS 5:6–8

If asked to list ten of your negative traits, you would probably just take a couple of minutes. To a degree, every person suffers insecurity and harbors a low self-esteem. No matter how talented or smooth people may appear on the outside, they, too, have their shortcomings riveted to their brains. For many Christians, that problem is enhanced because we're so often reminded how far short of God's standards we fall.

But how quick are you at recognizing your genuinely good points and those areas of your life where you come close to God's standards? These special qualities might include something nice you did recently for a member of your family or a talent that you've excelled in at school. Also included might be your godly attitude that always tries to see the best in other people, a giving spirit, self-control, or a sense of humor.

Think *honestly* and *positively* about yourself, and then list ten of those traits in the space below. As you compile the list, remember that your value in God's eyes is so great that he paid a high price (by giving up his Son)—just so you might live together forever in heaven.

1. _____
2. _____
3. _____
4. _____
5. _____
6. _____
7. _____
8. _____
9. _____
10. _____

In the coming week, pursue, practice, and perfect these traits!

See also: John 3:16; 1 Corinthians 6:20; 1 Timothy 6:11–14

OUT OF DARKNESS

My God turns my darkness into light.

PSALM 18:28

Whenever I land at an airport at night, I think of the story told by James Dobson about a friend who piloted his single-engine airplane toward a small country airport as the sun dipped behind the mountains.

Dusk settled quickly and quietly, and as lights blinked on in houses below, the man could barely make out the airstrip in the distance. By the time he maneuvered his craft closer for a landing, the black pavement was indistinguishable from the black of night.

His little plane was not equipped with lights, and the airport employees had left for the day. There was no one he could even radio for help. Circling the dark airport again and again, he stared hard below in hopes of spotting the runway. But he saw nothing.

For two hours he droned back and forth above the deserted airport, hoping against hope that his gas wouldn't run out. Yet as the needle of the fuel gauge nosed to empty, he knew that at any moment he could plummet from the sky to a certain death. His heart beat loudly and he wondered what death would feel like.

As his panic clenched tighter, a miracle happened. Someone on the ground had heard the plane circling aimlessly in the dark and had guessed the pilot's predicament. Hopping into his car, the man flashed on his brights and raced back and forth to illuminate the airstrip. And then he parked his vehicle at the far end of the runway and let his beams of light guide the pilot down for a safe landing.

There have been many times when darkness has crept into my life and I have been enveloped in the kind of panic that gripped the errant pilot. Perhaps you know the feeling, too. You face a hopeless tangle of problems at home, school, and work. Your future

296

seems clouded. Favorite sins and bad habits nag at your mind. Maybe someone close to you has died or been divorced, throwing more shadows across your life. Everything seems black.

I've found it's at the blackest moments that God wants to light my path. That light may simply be the assurance that he's in control and will eventually work bad circumstances into positive results. While things may not always improve immediately, he enables us to see the light at the end of the tunnel.

See also: Deuteronomy 31:6–8; Psalm 112:4; Romans 8:28

SECOND CHANCE

You are a forgiving God, gracious and compassionate, slow to anger and abounding in love.

NEHEMIAH 9:17

Sitting in a corner of the locker room during halftime of the 1929 Rose Bowl game, a University of California football player named Roy Riegels clutched a blanket tightly around his shoulders and wept.

Moments earlier, in front of a standing-room-only crowd, he had recovered a fumble and sprinted toward the end zone. He thought it was his moment of glory. Everyone shouted his name as he galloped down the open field toward pay dirt. He was alone, except for a teammate who raced wildly after him. And just yards short of an apparent touchdown, his fellow team member made a lunging dive and tackled him.

"You've run the wrong way!" he shouted hysterically.

No one said much during the half-time break in the locker room—not even the coach who normally had a lot to say. About the only sounds were Riegels' sobs. He felt ruined, and could only imagine what the newspaper headlines would say, not to mention his friends and family.

Finally, just before the team again took the field for the second half, the coach simply said, "The same men who played the first half will start the second." Everyone but Riegels filed out. The coach repeated himself.

"But I could never face the crowd again," Riegels said, looking up from his corner hideaway. "I've humiliated the team; I've humiliated myself."

The coach wouldn't listen. Putting his arm across Riegels' shoulder, he said, "Go on out there now. The game is only half over."

Whenever I blow it badly—specifically, at those times when I feel that I have made the world's biggest mistake and feel ruined as a Christian—I think of Roy Riegels, his wrong-way run, and his tremendous coach. And I'm reminded that God's message to me is much the same.

No matter what happens in my life, God is always there, able and willing to give me a second chance, a third chance, a hundredth chance. The game isn't over yet.

See also: 2 Chronicles 7:14; Romans 8:1–2; Ephesians 1:7–8

SPONTANEOUS PRAISE

Since the creation of the world God's invisible qualities—his eternal power and divine nature—have been clearly seen, being understood from what has been made, so that men are without excuse.

ROMANS 1:20

To think you find God only in church is as absurd as thinking you can find art only in a gallery. Bricks and mortar can't hold him. He isn't confined to a building any more than drama is to the stage, music to the radio, or monkeys to the zoo.

Open your eyes and there he is! Right outside your bedroom window. You catch glimpses of heaven in flower petals, a child's smile, the light of the sun, puddle reflections, or a lover's embrace.

As Paul writes, "By taking a long and thoughtful look at what God has created, people have always been able to see what their eyes as such can't see: eternal power, for instance, and the mystery of his divine being" (*The Message*). His point: you don't need a church pew to experience God.

"If you have never heard the mountains singing, or seen the trees of the field clapping their hands, do not think because of that they don't," wrote McCandlish Phillips. "Ask God to open your ears so you may hear it, and your eyes so you may see it, because, though few men ever know it, they do, my friend, they do."

Spontaneous worship can erupt any time, any place ... as it did one bright summer day to a young East Coast musician. Walking along the Mohawk Trail in the Berkshire Mountains, he climbed a tower overlooking Connecticut, New York, and Massachusetts. The soft-edged mist of morning had burned off, and the sun cut a golden swath across the sky. Spread before him from horizon to horizon were sparkling lakes, tall trees, and the scent of little things growing.

He was so awestruck that he rushed down to his car, grabbed his cornet, and climbed back into the tower. Suddenly he began playing the instrument with all his heart—for his own pleasure, the enjoyment of passing hikers, and for the glory of God. He'd heard the mountains singing and wanted to join in accompaniment.

Some people will one day stand before God and try to excuse their lack of belief by saying, "I never knew you because I never darkened the doorway of a church."

"Nonsense!" God will probably snort. "Did you never take a walk, look into the star-spangled sky, hear a clap of thunder, or watch a tree catch fire at sunset? I surrounded you twenty-four hours a day with evidence of my love and glory. You were just too busy to notice."

See also: Psalms 96; 150; Isaiah 6:3

POINTS TO PONDER—GOD

Holy, holy, holy is the Lord Almighty; the whole earth is full of his glory.

ISAIAH 6:3

The remarkable thing about the way in which people talk about God or about their relation to God is that it seems to escape them completely that God hears what they are saying.

SÖREN KIERKEGAARD

We see God all around us: the mountains are God's thoughts upheaved, the rivers are God's thoughts in motion, the oceans are God's thoughts imbedded, the dewdrops are God's thoughts in pearls.

SAM JONES

All-wise. All-powerful. All-loving. All-knowing. We bore to death both God and ourselves with our chatter. God cannot be expressed but only experienced. In the last analysis, you cannot pontificate but only point. A Christian is one who points at Christ and says, "I can't prove a thing, but there's something about his eyes and his voice. There's something about the way he carries his head, his hands, the way he carries his cross—the way he carries me."

FREDERICK BUECHNER

The universe is centered on neither the earth nor the sun. It is centered on God.

ALFRED NOYES

The public has a deep respect for the amazing scientific advances made within our lifetime. There is admiration for the scientific process of observation, experimentation of testing every concept to measure its validity. But it still bothers some people that we cannot prove scientifically that God exists. Must we lift a candle to see the sun?

WERNHER VON BRAUN

Does God seem far away? Guess who moved?

ANONYMOUS

We must wait for God long, meekly, in the wind and wet, in the thunder and lightning, in the cold and the dark. Wait, and he will come. He never comes to those who do not wait. He does not go their road. When he comes, go with him, but go slowly, fall a little behind; when he quickens his pace, be sure of it before you quicken yours. But when he slackens, slacken at once; and do not be slow only, but silent, very silent, for he is God.

FREDERICK W. FABER

A God who did not regard this [our own worst sins] with unappeasable distaste would not be a good being. We cannot even wish for such a God—it is like wishing that every nose in the universe were abolished, that smell of hay or roses or the sea should never again delight any creature, because our own breath happens to stink.

C. S. Lewis

See also: Isaiah 64:8; Luke 1:37; Romans 8:31; 2 Peter 3:9–14